IDENTITY CRISIS

One woman's story of finding her identity through the struggles of life

By
Ereka Howard, M.S.
2022

Identity Crisis

One woman's story of finding her identity through the struggles of life

Ereka Howard, M.S.

First Printing: 2022

ISBN: 979-8-9860894-5-4

Ordering Information:

Special discounts are available on quantity purchases by corporations, associations, educators, and others. For details, contact the publisher at the email listed below.

U.S. trade bookstores and wholesalers:
Please contact info@businessofbooksmastermind.com.

DEDICATION

This book is dedicated to those difficult times in my life when I felt like giving up. Obviously since you're reading this book, I did not give up. The passages in this book were written during the tough times. Since then, coping with life's struggles have improved. My hopes are that after reading my book, you become comfortable with your struggles. It's the struggle that makes us stronger. I want to thank God, my family, friends, and true mentors for holding me accountable and believing in me. No more privacy. Until the next time...

TABLE OF CONTENTS

FOREWORD

"We know that trauma has a profound impact on our lives physically, mentally, emotionally, and spiritually, yet rarely do we talk openly about the way that trauma interrupts our ability to thrive in our relationships and in our lives. In this book, Ereka Howard blends personal stories of trauma with important tools for trauma recovery in a way that de-stigmatizes the journey to healing. Ereka is brave and bold in telling the truth about trauma and takes away the shame that can keep us stuck. I recommend this book for anyone coping with the aftereffects of trauma because it will help give you hope!"

-Dr. Christine Lynn Norton, LCSW, CCAT, CET, CCTP, Professor of Social Work, Texas State University

I
WAS
TRAUMATIZED

Trauma stinks! It smells like four dirty pigs locked up in a steam room!!! I know that makes no sense, but oh well. No one knew that the night before, you had a nervous breakdown. You slapped and hit yourself in the face over and over after getting frustrated about a situation. So, there I was, about to walk into the room and have to put on a smile just so that everyone could see happy-go-lucky Ereka. It was hard, but this is a natural response of mine. I guess this was a response to my frustration and stress. Later down the road, I found out that certain responses such as this happened way before I was an adult. Can you imagine how it feels to be responding like a child to a situation as an adult? I had not felt like this in years! I felt defeated and helpless because of something that I had no control over. Now, I know you're asking yourself, little sweet Ereka did this to herself? And my answer will always be "I sure did". According to good ole Google and many other research methods, the way I responded is characterized as a trauma response. As a child, I would believe that trauma only existed in those who were in the military. For example, when I heard the word trauma, my mind immediately pictured soldiers going into battle and then coming back home to their families. Not one time did I ever understand that children dealt with trauma also. Well, I guess I was one of them when I would not know how to control my emotions, or did something wrong and couldn't process them correctly.

Examples of common responses to trauma are:
- Feel as if you are in a state of 'high alert' and are 'on watch' for anything else that might happen.
- Feeling emotionally numb, as if in a state of 'shock'
- Becoming emotional and upset.
- Feeling fatigued.
- Feeling very stressed and/or anxious

My face was so sore that it hurt to touch it and waking up in the morning and having to go to the training took a lot out of me mentally and emotionally. Looking at my face in the mirror and seeing the bruises kind of made me feel like a psycho. As a child, this was something that I did to cope with my emotions. Imagine hitting yourself in the face constantly because you didn't know how to channel the pressures of childhood and adolescence. There were bruises all over my face and my head hurt so bad it hurt to smile.

Think about what I just said, "It hurts to smile."

I'll wait...

Have you ever been in a rough situation where you couldn't even smile?

Meet Marylyn, Marylyn is the type of person who can accomplish just about anything in life. She was your high school jock, college leader, and loved animals. Most of the people in her circle only know her as the girl who always had a smile on her face. Little did they know that she was struggling to hold it together during times of distress. It was like she would smile so much that she sucked at crying.

Marylyn arrived at the organization with a smile on her face and was ready to help the children and their families. She realized that I went through everything just to be able to help others and tell them how I made it through. It would be hard for me to tell someone else how to get through something without knowing how to get through it individually. I have always managed to stay strong for everyone else and be the weakest for myself. It's probably because it takes time for me to put my trust in others as compared to putting my trust in God. Sometimes we have to go back to the place where we had too much trust in things that are not stable. Imagine that you are in a field. Throughout adulthood, my trust began to waiver in people because of the lack of value I had for them. My trust in God became stronger and this continues to be my truth. Trusting God is so much easier than trusting people. It was a struggle for Marilyn to participate in the activities during training but she felt better after leaving. Marilyn will be back.

Marilyn was able to cover up the bruises with makeup. Sometimes we try to do this with our problems in life. We act like everything is ok when deep down inside it is not. You've just been

If we were to take the paint off the wall, what would it look like underneath? - Ereka Howard

covering it up with a temporary shield. It's like painting over scratch marks in a room. When moving out of a home, you have to prepare the room for the next person to live in. However, if we scratch over the paint hard enough, we will still be able to see the original scratch. No matter how many layers we use to cover up the previous marks. The only true way to cover up the scratches is to start over and rebuild. The process of preparing something new requires the entire thing to be torn down to be made new. The more paint we use to cover up something, the thicker the area where the scratch is will increase and get bigger because of each layer of paint.

I know you are asking yourself, "What in the world is she talking about?" Seriously, think about it, paint is used to cover up things that we do not want others to see. There are different shades of colors as well. As a child, I would go to the store with my dad to look for the paint to finish the house or something else. I think I was about seven or so years old (yes my memory is that good). I just loved going to the store with my dad no matter what it was that we needed to get. My mother would be out of town working or at home working. Either way, she was working trying to help the community as always.

Sometimes I would ask my dad how long we were going to be at the store and every time he replied, "As soon as I find what I am looking for."

Wow! Did you catch that? Let me explain, a lot of times when we are unable to recognize something or what we need, everything else is put on hold until we find it. In life, we have to realize that our patience helps us get what we want. It is like riding a bike. You do not just expect to learn how to ride a bike immediately when you get on it now do you? Well, it took me a while to learn how to keep my balance. Have you ever tried so hard to keep your balance and you felt like giving up? We have all been there in life to the point of not caring. You see, my dad never told me exactly what we were getting at the store. He just knew what he wanted and took his time to find it.

So, when I and my dad finally got home with the paint, he began to open each can of paint that he bought. Poured it into the pan and mixed them with a stick that he had laying around outside in the backyard or on the porch. Before my dad could begin painting, he had to sand the walls and peel off the old paint. Heck sometimes, the paint automatically fell off. He made sure that he got off all of the old paint from the wall or he would not be successful and need to start all over.

This is a statement that many of us do not think about when it comes to redefining ourselves. Sometimes we will do everything in our power just to mask what is really going on inside. There was a time when I would be so good at putting on a front until I met some pretty cool people that saw past my exterior smile and helped me smile inside as well... It is because of their continuous support and accountability that I am who I am today. As proof, I had a professor in my master's degree program that saw past me hiding behind a smile and began to hold me accountable. She knows who she is and hopefully, she will read this book and know how much I appreciate her kindness and support. I remember it like it was yesterday walking into my class thinking that I was just going to coast by. My instructor's first lesson was on self-care. Before arriving at class, I had just left work and barely made it on time. I guess you can say that I had stress written all over my face. She looked at me with the type of facial expression that will make you feel anxious.

She also was a public speaker. Every time she looked at me, it made me feel intimidated. Each time I looked away. She told us to put away our things and just focus on the present moment. I was thinking to myself, she is not even paying attention to me. Little did I know, her attention was on me the whole time. It took me a while to put my things away and I thought that she would keep talking while I was putting away my things. Well, she didn't. She literally paused smoothly into her sentence until I was able to participate.

Under my breath, I was thinking "Why is she so focused on me and what I am?"

Finally, I was ready to participate. She went on with the assignment of self-care. There was music playing in the background which helped set the mood. I recall her saying "just stop," she said other things in between but I was not listening because I was thinking about what I had to do after class and what happened at work. Repeatedly, she kept saying stop.

I was like, "Stop for what?"

She kept saying this because she realized I was not listening. I am thankful for her accountability.

"Commitment seals and provides stability within any relationship. You have a decision to make! The problem is not the problem but the Outlook/Reaction to the problem."

-Ereka Howard

Being diagnosed with major depression, ADHD, anxiety, and PTSD is no joke especially when you have lived your whole life believing that you were fine. There I was, sitting in class as though I would coast straight through the program, but on the other hand, I did not know all of this was going on. I had two choices: either accept it and move on or deny it and be stuck for the rest of my life. Now, I know you are thinking, how in the world can someone so positive have so many mental illnesses altogether? Growing up, I was not quite sure what it was. How was I supposed to know that I was silently struggling and did not have any support? I already did not know who I was as an adolescent let alone having these difficulties. Somehow, I managed to make it throughout life in a positive way by the grace of God. I didn't take any medications for my diagnosis until I was an adult. The following points below explain how these mental illnesses can contribute to a child's overall functioning.

• Given that anxiety disorders are chronic problems that commonly begin in childhood or adolescence, family factors during childhood are likely to have the greatest (if any) influence.

- Consistent evidence indicates that adults with anxiety, especially social phobia, are less likely to be married or in a regular relationship than non-disordered populations.
- Children from conflicted families whose parents divorced more than 2 years earlier showed relatively low levels of anxiety. In contrast, children whose parents did not divorce and were high in conflict showed the highest levels of anxiety.
- Clinically, there appear to be several advantages to including and incorporating parents into treatment for child anxiety.

Anxiety vs. Facebook and Religion

- Based on the social anxiety scale, we developed a measure of seven Facebook specific anxiety items. These items relate to performing Facebook activities such as commenting on posts, uploading pictures, and making status updates.
- Higher religiosity predicts lower use of the internet, although demographic factors seem to be more predictive of engagement with the internet.
- Those with friends from religious organizations tend to have higher role conflict and more Facebook-specific anxiety. In general, those who are more religious experience more Facebook-specific anxiety across the board and more social anxiety for those who have a conservative interpretation of the Bible.
- Individuals who are more religious in behavior and belief may feel they risk negative sentiment from their religious communities depending upon what they reveal about themselves on Facebook.

• Regarding religiosity, those who prefer a literal interpretation of the Bible, attend church more frequently, and pray more often have higher anxiety.

Sometimes it is difficult to get to a particular place in life because there are things that will try to distract us and keep us from reaching our best potential. Subconsciously, we can allow those things to shake us or make us. Either way, it is up to us to not allow these things to distract us from the overall goal. Throughout my life, I have been in seasons of discomfort because I would allow others to distract me from what I needed to do. It could be a phone call, text, or social media. I would be engaged in something important and suddenly, here comes a distraction. If we are not careful, those things can hurt us. Your potential to ignore those things requires intention if you want to be successful. Honestly, I believe that it comes my way more than ever because I allow it to. You can call it ADHD or ADD. Nonetheless, be very mindful of distractions.

"Know the difference if it's a distraction that is trying to stop what God has placed together. Be happy."

-Ereka Howard

Google defines a distraction as A thing that prevents someone from giving full attention to something else.

Distraction: Definition and Examples
• Ambient noise (passengers, crew, equipment)
• Noisy equipment due to malfunction.

- Active conversations with passengers and colleagues.
- Information overload from displays.
- Cell phone use (talking, texting, gaming, social media use)
- Mind-wandering, rumination.

Set boundaries and know that it is ok and you will make the right decision. I have faith in you! Don't try to please everyone because you never will be able to do so. Don't worry about things you cannot control. Know what's your responsibility and what's not. These are some things I would tell myself during times of discouragement. This was another time that I had to encourage myself.

"You have to handle this situation the way you play tackle football. Do what's best for you."

-Ereka Howard

"Don't let ANYONE try to make you feel guilty for ANYTHING!"

-Ereka Howard

RETURN
TO
SENDER

Marilyn was confused. It wasn't until she looked on the card and saw the text returned to sender. She looked at it once and recognized the writing on the top of the card. Her mother sent the card back to her. As soon as she realized it, she went outside and sat on the ground and called her father. She asked him several questions as to why it came back. He was not able to answer the question but she knew deep down inside who wrote it and why it came back. Marilyn immediately called another family member over the phone. They talked about the situation. She told me to let it go and that it was time for her to live her life and let it all go. She got off the phone with her and immediately began crying and getting anxious. She was heartbroken. Marilyn asked herself, why did my mom send back the card I sent her for Mother's Day. If you know Marilyn's mom, then you would understand her directness of sending the card back and it would not offend you.

She looked closely at the letter just to make sure I was seeing what I was seeing. It was rejection staring at her and she felt so stupid for sending her something. When Marilyn thought about it, inside of her head, she had already cut her mother off from her life telling herself that she would no longer receive anything from her. After realizing, she went back inside her home. That same night along with the mail she received from her, she also received a book from another author who used her story in his book. She found her story and began reading it. As she was reading it, she started to cry uncontrollably to the point where she found strength. With everything that was going on at that time, reading her story, brought back memories and flashbacks of what she went through as a child. She immediately grabbed her keys and left home. To make things worse, Marilyn drove to a cemetery and cried. Crying was a way for her to process what happened. It

provided encouragement and support. Marilyn didn't share with her friend what happened while sitting in the cemetery on the phone because she felt that he would not understand it so she decided to not share. As bad as she wanted to get angry, she couldn't because she was able to transform that anger into strength just as she did as a child. On another note, she cried out to God! For encouragement, Marilyn made a video on her phone hoping that it would provide a sense of motivation during the times of trouble phone.

Health Line defines rejection as the following: Most people experience rejection over things big and small at least a few times in their lives, such as:

- a friend ignoring a message about hanging out
- being turned down for a date
- not receiving an invitation to a classmate's party

- a long-term partner leaving for someone else

During this time, Marilyn realized more and more that it was time to let it go! It was after midnight when she finally went back home home. She thought to herself, tomorrow is a new day. We have all experienced rejection of some sort. It does not feel good at all and it can put us into a depression if we are not careful. Here are a couple of ways to handle rejection:

1. Accept it but don't become it.

2. Validate your feelings.

3. Look for the lessons.

4. Know your worth.

5. Have a backup.

6. Narrow down the fear.

7. Face your fear.

8. Avoid negative self-talk.

According to Psychology Today, there are ways to treat the psychological wounds rejection inflicts. It is possible to treat the emotional pain rejection elicits and prevent the psychological, emotional, cognitive, and relationship fallouts that occur in its aftermath. To do so effectively we must address each of our psychological wounds (i.e., soothe our emotional pain, reduce our anger and aggression, protect our self-esteem, and stabilize our need to belong). TED also states that we are still vulnerable to serious and more devastating rejections as well. When our spouse leaves us, when we get fired from our jobs, snubbed by our friends, or ostracized by our families and communities for our lifestyle choices, the pain we feel can be absolutely paralyzing. Whether the rejection we experience is large or small, one thing remains constant — it always hurts, and it usually hurts more than we expect it to. The question is, why? Why are we so bothered by a good friend failing to "like" the family holiday picture we posted on Facebook? Why does it ruin our mood? Why would something so seemingly insignificant make us feel angry?

Be Present

So there I was, sitting in my car just thinking about random things. Honestly, getting stuck in my own head for the most part. With everything that's going on around me, I still must maintain my smile and strength inside and out. When we feel like we can't go on in life, that's when we need to continue to push. Don't worry about how you feel, just do it. Don't think about it, just go for it and give it all you've got! It's going to be hard TRUST ME! Think about how far you've come. Remember when you went through that storm that nearly killed you? Think about this, aren't you still alive today? I've found that it's tough maintaining our smile when everything around us is horrible. You made it, didn't you? Guys, listen, I feel horrible right now but somehow, I managed to do something about it. I've said this before, sometimes we don't know our own strength until strength is all we have to depend on. Keep fighting because I'm depending on you. I'm counting on you to win this fight. I'm in this with you and you are not alone. Please don't quit. I believe in you.

I learned a lot about feelings and emotions during my master's program. Additionally, I was able to gain a deeper understanding of burnout, people-pleasing, and manipulation just to name a few. One thing is for sure, don't become dependent on giving to where it controls your life. For example, giving so much to someone or something can create a sense of inadequacy. We have the potential of feeling inaccurate about ourselves at times. Also, try not to take on things or responsibilities that are not yours to handle. Thoughts, feelings, and emotions are temporary things depending on the situation that change all the time. This statement gives clarity on how to handle things that go on around us. The battle is not yours to handle, and you should not force anything to happen that is not supposed to happen. Don't force or fight against the current. You will gain strength and struggle at the same time. Sometimes you just must go with the flow and trust yourself before trusting others. I remember several times in life when I would help so many people to where I forgot to help myself. I felt empty if I did not help someone or if I noticed that they were not happy. I would take on the responsibility of thinking that I can fix them and make them all better. Here's another moment that I had to encourage myself out of a ditch.

"Second chances are not given to make things right. But are given to prove that we could be better even after we fall."

-Ereka Howard

This is not my job and never will be. It's best to do what you can when you can and however you can while still maintaining who you are as a person. It is impossible to please yourself and the other person the same way at the same time. Focus on your happiness because that's where you will gain ground and strength. Your life and happiness are just as important as the next person and don t sell yourself short for someone else's life. You deserve happiness and joy but it's not going to happen unless you start within.

YOUR
LIFE
MATTERS

Everyone sees me as the most positive person there is. Truth is, I'm just as scared as the next person is about what the future holds. Sometimes I sit alone away from others thinking about my next move and how I will get there. How I'm going to effectively help the next person succeed. Recently, I was at the store after coming from a speaking event where I was told that it was canceled at the last minute. I was expected to speak but due to changes in the institution, it didn't happen. I was sitting at the store and noticed an elderly woman struggling to get her groceries to her car. At that moment I realized everything was going to be ok. Not too many people can say that when they are hurting, they will be able to help someone else in their struggle. It seems so easy for us to become stuck in our struggles that we lose sight of the peace that exists in our lives. We become so tied to our unhappiness that we forget to see the inner peace that is within. When you reach out to help someone in need, you should find some peace by providing a service to others. With that thought process in mind, I immediately got out of my car and began to assist the elderly lady with her groceries. I told her; I'll help her which inspired me. It's the little things in life that matter. Without any resistance, she opened her door and allowed me to assist her. While returning to my car, I felt at peace. It gave me so much peace inside. It felt good to forget about my small manageable emotional issues and take time to help someone else.

Emotional trauma:

It perceives things that trigger memories of traumatic events as threats themselves. Trauma can cause your brain to remain in a state of hypervigilance, suppressing your memory and impulse control and trapping you in a constant state of strong emotional reactivity. The energy of the trauma is stored in our bodies' tissues (primarily muscles and fascia) until it can be released. This stored trauma typically leads to pain and progressively erodes a body's health. Emotions are the vehicles the body relies on to find balance after trauma.

We all have traumatic experiences that stick with us throughout life. Well, another experience was coming that I didn't expect to happen. This experience was a result of a traumatic experience. Sometimes I try to control the outcome of events in my life, but it does not always happen that way. I am actually writing this portion of the book the night after my 3-day hospital stay. This situation just happened without warning, and it literally caused me to be rushed to the ER in an ambulance. This story is somewhat of a blur so bear with me because of not being coherent. Two nights ago, I was rushed to the ER in an ambulance just a little bit before midnight on

Halloween. My health insurance was about to be out from a previous job so I was a little careful about going. How did I end up in the ambulance? I will take you back to the very beginning. It first started as a simple offer from a family member. As I was coming back from a long drive outside of the city I lived in, I was trying to make it to a family member's home to attend to the responsibilities that I agreed to. In short, my responsibility was taken care of, so I decided to have a drink. Or two. For some reason, drinking became impulsive and like a race. No one was there but me and my responsibility. I had just gotten off a study group with a few of my classmates that are in my doctoral program. Relieved that I finished my assignment and the semester ending soon, I started drinking. The Jell-O shots were good and so were the straight shots. When I got ready for bed. I took my normal prescribed sleeping pill and went to bed. Wait, did I start drinking after or before I took my pill is the thoughts that were going on in my head after being released from the hospital. I honestly do not know. Sometimes triggers are unpredictable and this was the case for me. For instance, a veteran may have flashbacks while watching a violent movie. In other cases, triggers are less intuitive. A person who smelled incense burning during a sexual assault may have a panic attack when they smell the same incense in a store. Some people use "trigger" in the context of other mental health concerns, such as substance abuse or anxiety. In these cases, a trigger can be a cue that prompts an increase in symptoms. For example, a person recovering from anorexia may be triggered by photos of very thin celebrities. When the person sees these photos, they may feel the urge to starve themselves again.

I remember taking two and a half shots of eighty-proof alcohol along with my sleeping pill. I remember waking up off and feeling absolutely horrible. I also remember looking outside and it was dark all of a sudden. I didn't know what time it was or anything. My phone was completely dead with no charger. I couldn't find a charger. I remember vomiting in the bathroom several times and my heart beating very fast to where I could feel it as I placed my hand on my chest. My mind was racing. I tried to take a bath to regroup but unfortunately that did not work either. Nothing to eat in almost 2 days and my immune system was failing quickly. To calm down the racing thoughts I was having, I remember submerging my head under the water to silence my thoughts. I did this at least five times. I had the chills. The shower curtain fell at least two times after putting it back up. I finally had no strength to put it back up so there I was, sitting in the bathtub with no clothes on and the water completed turned to hot but I couldn't feel the water because everything inside of me was cold. I just wanted to feel better. I tried to drink water and would vomit. It did not help. There was a time when I remember trying to climb on top of the tub to put the shower curtain back up and saying out loud, "I am tired."

If you know me, this statement never comes out of my mouth whatsoever. I was completely disoriented; I didn't know what time it was. No one could reach me. With everything that was going on in my life, I felt like I had connected with heaven. Seriously, no lie. It was like God was giving me a flashback of my life and telling me what to do. I am honestly not sure, but it sure did make me reflect on the past few years of my life and my current issues. A family member then came home and found me in the bathtub and asked if they should call 911. With hesitation and consideration, I said I'm ok. Now let's remember that my insurance ran out on this same day! After almost an hour, he said no Im calling the ambulance. It was a bunch of back and forth until I finally gave in and stopped worrying about money. My health was more important at that time. As I was being carried off on the stretcher, I was still nauseous and had no strength. It took the EMS to help me get some clothes on. I was embarrassed! When I arrived to the ER, my body and my mind was struggling. I had a total of 6 IV's that had to be placed in me at different times. My labs were of a dead person according to the nurses at the hospital. It was as though my organs were trying to fail which then lead to me being transferred to the toxicology department at another hospital across town. Whew was I scared! Little did I know that drinking alcohol tends to lower the immune systems of those who have autoimmune issues. This was news to me but it was a blessing in disguise. So from that point on, drinking became irrelevant.

According to Good Therapy, a trigger is a reminder of past trauma. This reminder can cause a person to feel overwhelming sadness, anxiety, or panic. It may also cause someone to have flashbacks. A flashback is a vivid, often negative memory that may appear without warning. It can cause someone to lose track of their surroundings and "relive" a traumatic event. Triggers can take many forms. They may be a physical location or the anniversary of the traumatic event. A person could also be triggered by internal processes such as stress.

Here are a few tips for emotional healing:

1. Be yourself. You must be yourself. ...

2. Invent yourself. You come with attributes, capacities, and proclivities and you are molded in a certain environment. ...

3. Love and be loved. ...

4. Get a grip on your mind. ...

5. Forget the past. ...

6. Flip the anxiety switches off.

FACTS
VS
FEELINGS

There is a difference between facts and feelings when we are explaining a particular situation. From my personal definition, Facts are defined as something that happens and is real while feelings on the other hand are the emotions that we feel in response to something that happened to us. Setting ourselves outside of the situation can allow us to understand the truth of what is going on and allow us to process the situation that is occurring in front of us. Another way to think about it is to ask yourself, are my feelings accurate or is it a response to my individual thoughts, and can it be proven as true? Being able to separate the two will give us a better way of processing the situation when we are listening to someone or explaining something to ourselves. I learned a lot about reflecting on feelings while in my master's program.

What a bummer! I had to retake a class that delayed my graduation date. This was devastating. My expectation was altered. I had my timeline in mind but back to the subject, oh yes facts versus feelings. Ok, so I can only speak for myself on this subject. When I would have conversations with others, I would always have an unbalanced conversation with them. Unbalanced in a way that means I would listen to them which would also trigger my particular beliefs about the situation. Listening is also a key point to consider when understanding a particular situation. For example...

"If you immaturely do something then you'll prematurely birth something in return."

-Ereka Howard

An Interpersonal Re-routing

While driving to Austin, about fifteen minutes away from my destination, my mind was running like always about the situation I was in. Before getting to my destination, I had to make a stop. As I was driving, I put the address in my phone. The directions took me out of the way or so I thought. While I was driving, I noticed that the path chosen was far away from the highway. As I got closer to the highway, I noticed that there was traffic on the interstate. The whole time I was driving, there was no traffic. It was right at that moment when I realized I should shut my mouth and stop being so negative about the current situation I was in. I guess you can say that I compared my situation to the traffic. Sometimes there will be detours that we have to take.

It might seem like it's leading to nowhere but eventually, it's only designed to protect us and prevent us from getting into bad traffic. When it all boils down to it, it's just a shortcut but it's not going to make sense while in the situation but eventually, you'll get to your destination. Just trust the process! It's going to work out. In life, we will have detours that will take us so far away from our goal but eventually, we will get where we are trying to go. Detours are designed to protect us or perhaps it is a shortcut. It will eventually get us to our destination. Trust the process, Ereka. Back to the story. It was at that very moment when God slapped me in my heart and mind and I had shut my mouth and my thoughts.

I said to myself, "Okay God, I hear you, you got jokes."

I said this under my breath and then all the racing thoughts calmed down. I would sike myself out to remain at peace in my head. What I was thinking was not a fact, it was a feeling that I had not only because of being held up or having to make a detour, it was my response to the situation.

Fighting Through Failure

Yesterday, I found out that I didn't pass the state licensing exam again. This was my second time taking the exam. When I did it the first time, it did not count. I failed both. I did a lot better on the second test but was only one point away from a passing grade. When I found out from the professor, I was at my internship location. I've only told a few people and I'm going to keep it like that for the simple fact that no one really has to know. Well, now I guess the world knows! Oh well. So back to the story...I failed it. I had plans to pass it and then take my licensing exam in the Fall. Can someone say, things don't always go as we planned!? Well, it didn't for me and I'm ok with it. I'll just keep fighting and studying so that when I take it in two months, I will be more prepared. The exam is never the same each time it is taken. Some questions are similar while others are totally different each time. These next few months, I'm going to plan my study time. I still don't know what's going to happen but I am praying that I pass! I will pass. I said this the first time and I'll say it again, I'll pass. Period. Either way, I'll stay focused and not give up. It's time to go into overdrive. I'm still debating if I should get back on social media. I haven't been on in two full months and I'm still okay with it. My days are extremely long with little to no time to play. I didn't really have a summer break like everyone and that's ok too. I'm not everyone and everyone is not me. Now that I have to retake the exam, it is time to hit the ground harder!! Throughout everything that has transpired within the past few years, I am still able to stay focused on writing this book. Taking the exam and being one point away from a passing grade is partially why I have decided to title it, One Point Away. I almost passed with one point away!

Job Losses

Have you ever lost a job before? How did you feel about losing it? The more I lose, the stronger I feel. Each time I get discouraged, the more I end up remembering what else I've been through. If God did it before, he will provide it again. I don't know how or when but all I have to lean on is what he did before. I can't get discouraged and I can't get sad. I did exactly this, but it's hard for me to stay that way. The quicker you move, the quicker God will move. Don't lose who you are. Stay grounded in the person God has developed you to be. Everything you have ever accomplished in life, God has made it possible.

From sunup to sundown, I was worried and anxious about not having a full-time job because I struggled mentally and emotionally not knowing how things were going to turn out. I had mixed emotions about the whole thing over and over until it caused me to worry and stress. I fasted and prayed for several weeks because I wanted God to do something supernatural on my behalf. I went to the gym to work out. There were times when I didn't eat before working out! I sweated, prayed, and pushed myself to the limit! I was tired and worn out but I kept moving forward while trusting God, day in and day out, minute by minute, and second by second. It was hard, but I kept fasting and will continue to do so. It's a job trying to look for a job!!

Each week was a struggle to get through. The more I thought about it, the more anxious I became. Each rejection became more difficult to handle. It was when I learned to accept the fact that I could not tell the future. All I could do was take one step at a time.

When I thought I could and things turned out the opposite, it put me in a worse situation and I became frustrated and discouraged not knowing how or what the outcome would be. When I struggled, I thought the circumstances were too stressful and I couldn't be making the situation worse in my mind. I would think that this week I'm going to get blessed and when it didn't happen I became frustrated. I tried to control it and tell God when He was going to do something. I had to step back and let Him work everything out. Over and over, week after week, day after day, minute by minute it became difficult to handle.

Well, I just lost my job again and I wasn't even there for 90 days! They said it was because of the requirements for the notes. I was crushed but kept it together. It was unexpected. I left and called my spiritual mother. I cried so hard while driving home and on the phone with her until I got dizzy while driving home. When I got out of the car I still felt dizzy and tried walking up the stairs. This loss hit pretty hard. The experience sucks and I did not know what to do. I thought this job loss period of my life was over! Apparently not. I hadn't eaten in almost two days! I was on sleeping pills three times a day, 100 mg trazodone, muscles relaxed, and hydrocodone, applying for jobs even out of state. In bed, out of it!! My eyes were bloodshot, and I had not showered but maintained my hygiene. I haven't taken pills in over seven years! Suicide and depression are real. Depression feels like giving up and not wanting to keep going. Ultimately, you just want everything to stop and you're tired of starting over. It took me a long time to be motivated to eat. I lost at least ten pounds since finding out about my job. I contacted everyone from my past to find employment. did everything! I found myself sleeping and laying in the bed not wanting to do anything but apply for jobs. I've gotten interviews and no response at all. Day by day, minute by minute, and second by second something had to give in Jesus' name! There was a series of unfortunate events. I failed my exam, had personal life issues, and two weeks later I lose the same job that I got hired on to start my license. It was a Christian based, non-profit organization and that made it worse. I didn't pass. My coping skills need to improve! They specifically told me not to worry and that it'll come easy and don't worry. I wasn't even 90 days into my job when they told me that the relationship had to be relinquished. I was confused. Despite my employer telling me not to stress about learning everything, I did everything in my power to learn it. When I was getting the hang of everything, they terminated me during my grace period. It hurt my feelings and I kept on telling myself that it was still a job. According to American Psychological Association, depression is defined as the following:

○ Feeling sad or having a depressed mood

○ Loss of interest or pleasure in activities once enjoyed

○ Changes in appetite — weight loss or gain unrelated to dieting

○ Trouble sleeping or sleeping too much

○ Loss of energy or increased fatigue

○ Increase in purposeless physical activity (e.g., inability to sit still, pacing, hand wringing) or slowed movements or speech (these actions must be severe enough to be observable by others)

○ Feeling worthless or guilty

○ Difficulty thinking, concentrating, or making decisions

○ Thoughts of death or suicide

Professional Job Loser

When I graduated from college with my bachelors degree, I was homeless and it was extremely hard for me to find a job. I did anything and everything just to make ends meet. I did not ask my parents for anything and it was by the grace of God that I made it through! I lost so much weight and was a mess during this time in my life. I know my current situation is not my final destination, but

it triggers me to the point of losing hope and faith in myself and God. Moving out of my parents house at the age of 18 was a good thing but it left me with the decision to live my life based on my experiences. After my bachelor's degree, I decided to not go back home and live with my parents. It was only supposed to be for a couple of months until I got on my feet. Even after then, I was able to rent out a room for free. After college, I didn't have my own place until about 5 years later. I'm thankful she did. When we finished our conversation, she said she did it because she didn't mind helping out a friend with a good heart. I was under so much pressure because I was not supposed to stay as long as I did with her.

Every day was stressful and some nights I had to wait in my car just until she got home because she was busy and I didn't want to be a burden but thank God she was ok with being used by God. She said she is doing well and working at Apple. Thank you Jesus for using her. It was a rough season for me and still impacts me. I'm working on my self-care. God is in control even when we cannot see him.

Call me crazy, but this is how I get through my days when waiting on a job offer or interview. It's the truth! Or I will stay busy throughout the day or plan ahead and do my best to live in the moment and do my absolute very best! It made me a better person too. Depression set in and my day went well, but now reality hit me hard and I couldn't stop crying so I went to my room and lay in the bed. I was going to go to the gym and I even eat a little bit today but now, we'll know it is a reality and I might take my sleeping pills. I was empty and I did not have anything left in me.

With three interviews next week, I am hopeful and nervous. My hope is that I will land a successful job within the next two weeks. In Jesus's name. Amen. Either way, I have to keep moving forward. I'm able to eat today. I'm trying to live in the moment. I contacted my friend last night who allowed me to sleep on her couch.

> *What's GOING ON IN YOUR HEAD IS NOT THE TRUTH!*
>
> *-Ereka Howard*

While headed back home from out of town I was wondering how I was going to make ends meet with no income other than possible unemployment benefits. Maybe they didn't want to wait 90 days for me to grasp the job? What made them fire me and is it true? I'm curious because they said they would work with me and lead me to believe something that was not true? Maybe it's my fault, I mean everything! I've had several interviews this past week and some positives and negatives but I still had some. I don't know what God is doing but I must trust him. If it was due to conduct of when you went to get your hair done on your lunch break (phone was not working properly) you even communicate with them and discussed with them (She) and responded to the email mentioning that your phone was not working and you and she experienced it not working, you replied to the email stating the situation after the fact, they didn't mention anything and she wanted you to schedule your clients after the fact and you even called her during the fact and she said to not worry about it. You offered your apologies and figured it was a miscommunication. You worked almost an entire week until they decided to separate. If it was because of this, they didn't mention it during the separation. You communicated ongoing and sent text messages and even other co-workers were doing this. Ereka, you know you didn't mean any harm IF THIS WAS THE CASE for separation. Trust God Ereka and don't feel any guilt. You didn't screenshot or think anything of it after because she understood at least that's what you got after the conversation. It was not even mentioned during the team meeting that you were going to be terminated (occurred after) You received a call from unemployment benefits stating that your benefits could be terminated. Why? Oh lord here we go. Ereka, don't let the situation control you.

As I was applying for unemployment, the customer service representative said that I have to be strong and do something about what you are going through. She said that God is going to bless you for what you did. My unemployment benefit was stopped and I've been fasting. I'm tired. I'm crying. I'm drowning. I'm lost. I'm hurt. I'm confused. I have no job. I have to be out of my apartment in a few weeks. My bills are due. No income. I'm reaching out and people are wanting to help me. I have to be strong. This hurts. I'm in my apartment. During this time I made several sacrifices and my experience is below.

I've applied to over 50 jobs. Had interviews. Been rejected jobs. Several. No callbacks. Time is wasted. I'm praying. FASTING. trying to hear from God. Trying to have faith. Trying my best to not lose my mind. I'm lightheaded. I want to quit. How do you keep moving forward with nothing changing? I'm expecting things to change when I make decisions. I'm trying to not take pills. Good days and bad. I'm discouraged. I have to start packing my things and it will trigger me to think that things are not going to change and I'm starting from the very beginning. I'm tired. I have to control my thoughts. Negative and positive. My expectations are not being met. I surround myself with gospel music. Day in and day out. I try to stay busy. I'm discouraged. I'm worried that I'm going to fail. I'm depressed. I feel like a burden on people and I'm supposed to have all the answers and be positive. It's hard. I don't even want to write this stuff. I am even though. I can't afford my bills. My phone's battery is bad. Goes from 100% to 5% in seconds. Did it last night. My phone bill has not been paid. My phone might get cut off. Should I start packing? But what if I'm making the situation Worse and not supposed to be? How do you plan ahead when you have no plan? Faith? Faith in what? Who? God? Or myself? I'm lacking in both areas. I curled up in a ball on the floor. I had a therapy session today and missed it because I didn't know the correct time. Don't make it your emotions I said to myself. Let the situation remain the situation. Remember what your counselor said during your session. I don't know where to apply for jobs because my apartment lease is up in July. This is discouraging and scary. No constant income and the Texas Workforce Commission contacted me about my benefits today. While speaking with my grandmother about what's going on in your life and she started to talk about how her life was when you were a baby how she had to struggle a lot and how far she has gotten in her. Think about how far and the things she went through growing up and how things were for her in Cuba with her family and in America. She gave you a lot of encouragement and motivation (in Spanish) for 15 minutes. If your grandmother can make it then so can you. Go Ereka!

It's like we believe God for the same thing that ends up disappointing us!! For example, you apply for a job and get the interview then you're still believing them for that same thing during the process until when the same thing you believed ends up not being what you believed in then the Job ends up not being what you believed in because they don't want you for the job. Today is way better than yesterday. Today I went to the SNAP office to take care of my food stamps.

It's Saturday and my birthday is Sunday and I didn't want to be alone is what I was feeling at the time. It was stressful, and I was praying and hoping that my interviews set up this week would be successful and I would get a job quickly. My intuition told me to check my bank account. I reluctantly did it. Expecting it to be less than what my bills required, I looked at my account and it was almost double what I thought it would be. I looked at it again and was baffled. I checked my account before we left and knew how much money I had in my account and all of a sudden there was extra money in my account. I'm so thankful for God and I know he'll take care of me. This was proof. I barely spent money on my trip because I knew it was the beginning of the month and the rent was due along with my car payment. I am thankful and I pray my interviews are successful in Jesus' name. The money deposited in my account was my last check from the company that let me go. Eeek! got back so

I'm leaving it to my brothers to stay with for a couple of days. God, I trust you and sometimes I don't feel the trust or even you but I'm still leaning on you. I've been told to get out and sometimes I do and sometimes I don't because I need to save every penny I have at this time. I'm sure it'll work out for my good but I don't know when. God, I love you and I need you. It's been three weeks since the separation from my previous job and it's been a living hell. God, I want to go to church to get healing but I can't because I need to save every penny. So, that's why I'm going to my brothers. I haven't gone anywhere or done anything other than going to the gym once and to my interviews because I need to save every penny for my bills. I might go to the gym and come back home. Who knows. I hope it doesn't hurt my pocket with all the driving.

I pray that I am exaggerating about everything that's going on, but I'm able to manage my thoughts and there I was, sitting in my car at the gym contemplating whether I should go inside or not. It's been weeks since I went to the gym after my depression. I am usually in the gym every week. It was a rainy day and several tornadoes were in the area. Not knowing what tomorrow would bring, I went inside anyway. I can barely afford a gym fee and the money was coming out of my bank account. I'm ignoring the way I feel and what I'm dealing with. Did I mention that I contacted the supervisor that fired me to see if I could get my personal folder that I mistakenly gave when the "transition" occurred? I have 6 miles left in my gas tank. I didn't want to but, I had to release the hurt and bad feelings I was dealing with because it was holding my life hostage. I was hurt and I had to be okay with the hurt. I'm still unemployed but I'm still breathing. The morning started rough and it lasted through the afternoon. This morning I was rushing to the food stamp office which was already weighing heavily on me. While driving there, I got stopped by the cops for speeding. nerves and anxiety were extremely high. I had an interview for what I thought was a full-time position. Later, I found out it was part-time and it is not guaranteed hours or paid. I have to pay for my onboarding! They hired me, but at this time I cannot pay for anything that I can't afford. I need a job and more importantly, income. There I was crying in front of the officer and of course, I was at fault and now I have an additional bill to pay on top of everything else! This sucks, I thought to myself. A lot is going on at one time!

The Re-Routing Intersection Creates Obstacles

Rejection most frequently refers to the feelings of shame, sadness, or grief people feel when they are not accepted by others. A person might feel rejected after their significant other ends a relationship. A child who has few or no friends may feel rejected by peers. According to google. The story below explains a time when I felt rejected. Our feelings are temporary.

So, while crying like the ugly cry like really really bad, I lost my voice due to me screaming so much when I got my ticket due to being so overwhelmed at that time. I took several. minutes in between my breakdown to get everything in control. Again, this is a trauma response. I had an interview a couple of hours later. Other things went on and I had that on top of that! It was a rough day! I finally went to apply for food stamps and almost started crying because I never thought I would have to do this. They told me to come back in the morning because the line was long. I told them I would. Before I knew it, I was in my car heading home trying to figure out how I could do self-care. When I got home, I looked in my messenger and didn't realize I had booked a Skype call with a radio station. I took medicine to calm my nerves before and knew that the call would be horrible not only because I barely had a voice but because I had to take the chance. I hope the lady understands. I told her that the next time we talk she will have good content (I'll be able to tell her what's happening now) I hope I made a good decision.

> *Remember that you're not a bad person for having these thoughts. You can't control every irrational thought that pops into your head.*
>
> *– Ereka Howard*

Most people experience unwanted thoughts, but how you deal with them affects your experience. For instance, if you choose to believe an irrational thought, it can cause more anxiety and worry. You will most likely have another irrational thought following the first one, and so on. The cycle can be endless if you don't manage your reactions to your thoughts. Anyone can experience irrational thoughts, and most of us do from time to time. This is especially true for people who are prone to worrying, overthinking, and stress. Certain mental health conditions, such as those that cause paranoia or obsessive behavior, can cause irrational thoughts as well.

I've never done this before and I feel guilty. Oh, and by the way, my birthday is in two days. Happy birthday to me!!!!! Sarcastically speaking! I plan to sleep the entire day!!!! I only ate two boiled eggs today and drank water. I took sleeping pills after my interview. This is how I spent my birthday lol..I would think about my life 2 weeks in advance about my situation which would cause me to stress more not knowing the future and not wanting to wait or look forward to the next two weeks. I would overanalyze everything which is overwhelmingly bad for my mental health. I feel so alone with having to take care of everything that's going on in my life physically mentally, emotionally, and especially FINANCIALLY! I'm in bed alone listening to worship music with a few tears. My heart is heavy because I don't know what the future holds and my birthday is tomorrow. But there's a lot on my mind, heart, body, and spirit that is not right--but God still loves me.

Constant worrying, negative thinking, and always expecting the worst can take a toll on your emotional and physical health. It can sap your emotional strength, leave you feeling restless and jumpy, cause insomnia, headaches, stomach problems, and muscle tension, and make it difficult to concentrate at work or school. You may take your negative feelings out on the people closest to you, self-medicate with alcohol or drugs, or try to distract yourself by zoning out in front of screens. Chronic worrying can also be a major symptom of Generalized Anxiety Disorder (GAD), a common anxiety disorder that involves tension, nervousness, and a general feeling of unease that colors your whole life.

I feel so alone and unworthy. I feel so guilty for doing it but I have to get out of this environment because of what's going on in my life (depression with my job loss etc.). It took a lot to make the decision but I have to do it for myself. I'm so disconnected and disappointed in myself that it's not even funny. Did I make a bad decision by accepting the job? But if God didn't want me there, he would have not opened the door. I disagree and I'm feeling guilty. At this present moment, I take full responsibility for my actions. Maybe I stressed them out by the stress that I was dealing with at home? Maybe I was so stressed out after not passing my LPC exam that I worked so hard to pass and didn't? Maybe they didn't believe who I said I was?

Obstacles

Try not to "push" the thoughts out of your head or punish yourself for having them. Try not to argue with the thought or belief, either. Simply notice the thought and accept that it is present. When you resist the thought, you give it more power. When you tell yourself *not* to think of something, for instance, you are much more likely to think of it. It may be difficult, but try to let some time pass. Don't let your irrational thoughts disrupt what you are doing. Let yourself feel your worry, stress, or anxiety, but try to observe your feelings instead of reacting to them right away. Here are some examples of how to reframe your irrational thoughts.

Irrational Thoughts examples

• The store employee is looking at me right now because they think I'm sad and pathetic.

• This plane is experiencing turbulence. The pilot hasn't said anything yet which probably means we're going to crash.

• I'm going to have a panic attack in public and people will think I'm crazy. **Reframed Thought**

• The store employee just glanced at me because I entered the store. I can continue shopping here.

• Turbulence is normal on an airplane. I'll follow the flight attendant's instructions and stay in my seat until it passes.

• I'll practice some deep breathing until I feel better. If I need to, I can go home early.

TRUE
OR
NOT

I don't feel like going to the gym is what I said when I was walking out the door this morning. I don't feel like being around anyone or putting on a front like everything is all gravy. Knowing this, somehow, I managed to get my clothes on and drive almost 30 miles just to go to a spin class. My mind, heart, body spirit, and soul are exhausted and I didn't eat or drink anything before going to the gym. I'm subconsciously living day to day right now and have been for the past few weeks. I'm depressed. I arrived at the gym and I almost fell asleep at the wheel. I was so sleepy that when I arrived, I was listening to an Eric Thomas audio message titled "Stop empowering the problem."

Emotional overwhelm is a state of being beset by intense emotion that is difficult to manage. It can affect your ability to think and act rationally. It could also prevent you from performing daily tasks. Emotional overwhelm may be caused by stress, traumatic life experiences, relationship issues, and much more.

After it went off, meditation music came on and I fell asleep in my car for about 5 minutes. I've never been this tired when coming to the gym. What is this?? Oh well, I'm going inside to wait for class to start. Here we go! I reached back in my seat to get a snack I had. It's a peanut butter power bar. I'll eat a bite. I have to use the bathroom. Ok bye. Fred Hammond's" They that wait for" song was on when I was getting out of my car. I told myself and was able to keep going when hearing this song. Come on Ereka, you got this!

I've moved on Physically but truth be told, I haven't mentally and emotionally. I'm thinking about sending out an email also to the CEO of the organization asking why they relinquished our relationship. This will be sent to not get anyone in trouble, but to honestly know what I did wrong and so that I could fix it. I have taken full responsibility and maybe I self-sabotaged everything. I'm not sure but whatever I did, I want to make it right. One thing I learned while being unemployed was that I had to take one day at a time literally because I didn't know when I was going to become employed full time but each day was totally different. I had my expectations of when it was going to happen and with whom but sometimes it didn't happen like that so the only way that I could have peace with the situation was to realize that I'm not in control.

What are your positive affirmations? Take some time to fill them out below. While considering them, think about a time when you had to make a big decision about something that caused you to be discouraged. You got this!!

1.

2.

3.

4.

5.

One way to release guilt is by expressing your feelings in a journal and actually seeing your thoughts on paper. This is also a wonderful way to get thoughts down and then circle back with them to remind yourself how much you've achieved over time.

"My fears got the best of me which also caused insecurities and unmet expectations."

-Ereka Howard

Let's journal while considering these questions:

1. **Where does your guilt come from? Guilt is not yours to accept. It's an internal fight. If you can think back to the last time you felt guilty, what caused it?**

2. **Who is the main person in your life that causes you to feel guilty?**

3. **How can you forgive yourself?**

4. How has guilt affected your life?

_____

_____

_____

_____

_____

_____

_____

Here are some simple ways to do instill stronger willpower:

● Live your life according to a purpose that motivates you to get up and move on with life.

● Remember that it doesn't always have to be about money. We know that you'd like to pay the bills but doing something that you love is better than becoming a corporate machine.

● Stop holding grudges and moaning about how unsatisfactorily your situation is. You can write your own story by forgetting the past and working on your future. ● Stand by your values and opinion and don't let them dissolve in the rat race. This will help you to have lesser regrets and guilt-ridden days.

● Always get up after you fall. Know that failure is part of life and change can occur at any moment.

Tomorrow is my session with my therapist along with another interview. I spent a lot of time with God today and I don't know when I'm going to get a job, but I just know something is going to become available. I will remain happy during uncertainty. I am grateful for God's grace. Waiting for jobs to call either with interview offers after being denied is difficult. I tried to stay busy, especially during my times of fasting. My expectations are not God's. I interviewed with and for jobs that I did not even apply for and when I got an interview, I either became insecure about the job or possessed a discouraging mindset about the outcome. I sabotaged the opportunity in my mind but was able to still move forward and stay consistent regardless of what the employers thought about me. I acknowledged the opportunity and did my best during the entire interview regardless of how I felt so ultimately, I could give myself credit for doing my best and going with God's plan, good or bad. I prayed even when I told myself I wouldn't. I fasted until the interviews and didn't eat anything because I wanted to show God how much I was sacrificing for the opportunity. I even didn't eat after the interview to push myself. I fasted because I thought God would not bless me with what I wanted and this happened even when I fasted for something and didn't even get what I wanted. I had to realize that even during my intense fasting, God still saw my sacrifices, and if he didn't give me what I wanted I knew he still loved me and wants the best for me. Just because I did something hard, it doesn't mean God didn't see it. When fasting, God is not focused on the duration of time, he is focused on the quality with him and the trust placed in him during trials and tribulations. I interviewed for jobs that I didn't even apply for and still moved forward even though I didn't know what to expect. God remains in the miracle-working business. This proved to me that He is still working on my behalf and I should stay encouraged. All things work together.

WHY DO WE FAST?

The following are reasons why we fast. Take some time to reflect on the scriptures that go along with the explanations. Feel free to grab a piece of paper and write down your need for fasting.

1. To prepare for ministry. Jesus spent forty days and nights in the wilderness fasting and praying before He began God's work on this earth.

2. To seek God's wisdom. Paul and Barnabas prayed and fasted for the elders of the churches before committing them to the Lord for His service (Acts 14:23).

3. To show grief. Nehemiah mourned, fasted, and prayed when he learned Jerusalem's walls had been broken down,

4. To seek deliverance or protection. (Ezra 8:21-23).

5. To repent. After Jonah pronounced judgment against the city of Nineveh, the king covered himself with sackcloth and sat in the dust.

6. To gain victory. After losing forty thousand men in battle in two days, the Israelites cried out to God for help. Judges 20:26

7. To worship God. Luke 2 tells the story of an eighty-four-year-old prophetess named Anna.

The Re-routing is OK

I went to them with a hopeful mindset and heart. I spoke with Unemployment Benefits, and they stated that my most recent job has not responded regarding the separation from employment and has until midnight to do so. My account is being investigated and if they do not respond, then unemployment will make a decision. Either way, God is in control in Jesus's name. God, cover and protect my character, reputation, identity, and outlook personally, professionally, mentally, physically, and emotionally. I spoke with unemployment benefits. She gave me this information just now. It is almost time for my counseling session. It's amazing how we allow certain stories to remain on replay in our minds— when they are not based on reality. I tend to want something so much to the point that I will overthink it. For example, when I am dealing with something, my expectations will replay in my mind. It gets so bad that I must ground myself and think about what's in front of me. As soon as I think of a thought that takes control over me, I immediately stop that thought and come back to reality. God help me! Not to say that reality is bad, but my thoughts tend to be out of control sometimes, especially during a depressive episode. I think the worst about the situation and sabotage everything without and even myself. It becomes a fight between what is true and what's not true. At times I had to subconsciously do something while a negative thought was in my head. It is hard to fight myself when I'm in a battle with Myself. I am on my way. Everything is going to be okay is what I said. I have to push myself even when I'm completely drained and discouraged. I go to the gym

"I cannot allow anything or thought to control my entire life which is hard especially when I am going through it."

-Ereka Howard

48

and just for that time, I work out, and pushing myself during my workout inspires me and gives me strength because I lift weights or run with uncomfortable motivation at the same time.

I realized that no matter where I was physically, I must be strong mentally and emotionally as well. Life is more than what we have or what we do. It is who we are inside that defines us and what we do with it.

LESSON
LEARNED

I am required to be out of my apartment in two weeks. I do not have a job and I made plans to move in with my brother. I'm hopeful and grateful for everything. I am going to the gym on a Sunday because I refuse to start the week off on a negative note. Tomorrow I'll be interviewing with the company that I left before becoming unemployed. Receiving my counseling license will confirm a lot of things in my life legally. There are a lot of people who unethically practice with the degree but I will not be one of them. When I didn't pass the first time, I thought that I was it made me feel incompetent about some of the things that I learned throughout my master's program. This was discouraging and caused me to feel insecure about what I knew. I had mixed emotions about what I studied. It took deep meditation and personal gratification and assurance that has to be acknowledged within myself to believe that the things I was thinking in response to my exam were a lie and that I was just as valuable as a clinician when I graduated compared to when I graduated and before I took my licensing exam. It was tough for me to believe in myself, and I had to believe in myself and the person

God has ordained and called me to be. I am not perfect and I know he has a plan for me. It feels lonely when I have developed a personal plan for My life that has not been met. I must keep loving myself and moving forward—by ultimately becoming secure in who I am. It's lonely but I have to have faith and strength. When I was alone and no one was there for me, I had to fight to keep going and believe in myself. It took close to a year to do so. I have to fight through what's happening in front and around me, especially when something didn't go the way I expected. At times, I will lose Myself to the point where depression and lack of abilities are tested.

Symptoms of depression include a depressed mood (feeling sad, empty, or hopeless); lack of interest or pleasure in activities that I used to enjoy; fluctuations in weight; difficulty with sleeping; low energy; feeling worthless; feeling guilty; difficulty concentrating; difficulty making decisions; feeling irritable; feeling restless; and/or feeling suicidal. The symptoms of depression make it difficult to function in day-to-day life. As symptoms become increasingly unmanageable students may even begin to feel suicidal... According to research, suicide is the second leading cause of death for individuals aged 15- 34. Anyone who is feeling suicidal needs to know that this is a major symptom of depression and does not have the skills to cope with suicidal feelings alone. With help, I too can get relief and feel better. Traditionally, when we think of trying to manage depression, we think of engaging in therapy or taking medication. Why am I mentioning this? Well because depression can lead to suicidal behaviors unintentionally. While those things are helpful and are often recommended for anyone with clinical depression, many other things can also be helpful that are sometimes overlooked. Additionally, there are many ways to deal with depression that have better long-term outcomes (and lower relapse rates) than psychotherapy or medication alone. Many of the ten coping strategies listed here go hand in hand and can build on each other, incrementally increasing My overall sense of well-being. For example, if I am exercising and eating well, I will also likely be sleeping well. We hope this list will offer effective strategies for dealing with depression in college. No one should cope with depression alone. Trained and licensed mental health professionals can provide support in helping me to find relief from My symptoms. Psychotherapy can help individuals identify what issues are contributing to their symptoms of depression and how best to address these issues. As the reports, psychotherapy can help reduce symptoms of depression and prevent future episodes of depression.

There are many things to consider when choosing a therapist, the outlines several factors I might want to take into consideration, such as the type of psychotherapy or specialties that the therapist offers. Additionally, research has shown that the relationship between the therapist and the client is central to positive change in therapy. If I have been to therapy before and did not find it helpful, do not assume that it can't ever be helpful. It may be that the therapist was not a good fit for me.

One symptom of depression is a feeling of worthlessness or excessive guilt. Sometimes when we feel worthless or guilty we have a tough time setting boundaries in our best interest because we are more worried about what the other person wants or needs than what we want or need. This is information that was gathered while doing personal research within this area. This happened to me a few times.

Setting good boundaries is like setting good goals. We recognize that we can only do so much, so we make a conscious effort to try to commit to the things that fill us up and bring us joy. This may mean choosing to go for a long run and then going to bed early instead of going to a party that My friend wants me to go to. . It can be hard to disappoint people by saying no or setting a boundary especially if we already feel inexplicably worthless or guilty. This is also the behavior of a people-pleasing person. However, many people find that when they push themselves to say no or set a boundary, even though it feels hard in the moment, they experience a boost in self-esteem and feelings of self worth after doing so for tips and strategies for saying no and setting boundaries. Boundaries are important when working with others in need.

It's happening to me, and I must fight through it so tough that I am not aware of what I've done. It is at this point that I should just get up and fight.

Honestly, I don't think I got where I am right now because I decided to quit even when I wanted to give up. I might feel like My life is not valuable and not feel appreciated by others, but I must have a personal and internal drive inside of me that says I can make it. When it boils down to it, it is only going to be me in the coffin when My time is up. Just because I am financially or physically healthy, does not mean I am mentally healthy. My brain disrupts everything and causes problems. While I have been helping everyone else succeed in life, I've been hurting Myself to fail. It's time to pick Myself up, fight, and do for Myself just as I have done in the past. It's not being selfish, but having self-worth. It's time to stop looking at others succeed while I just sit there and die. Let that be something that shows how much I do have within me. Switch it up Ereka, change the game, and don't feel bad about it. " Others will try to put guilt on me so that it can cause me to stop progressing in life but, don't listen. Don't ever put My life in the hands of others is another thing I said to encourage myself.

"This is another time when I had to encourage myself when something happened that I disagreed with. Self-motivation is one of the most powerful things we can ever have in life."

-Ereka Howard

Mentorship

I don't depend on others to help me succeed. Whether in or out of a relationship, I take responsibility for my internal actions relating to being with others or being alone. In other words, use the way I respond to insecurities, setbacks, or incompetence, and build my strength up so that I can be happy during the tough times internally and externally. I was in my car texting my spiritual father/ pastor who's been knowing me for years. I was sitting at my desk at work thinking that I could handle it when I couldn't. I was texting him how I felt about my life out of anger and discouragement. The last I received read, "Don't hold it in" which is something that I tend to do a lot but have learned to let out my emotions go. I'm glad my spiritual father told me this. This spoke volumes in my spirit and that is exactly what I tend to do. I act like everything is okay which causes me to keep the stuff inside because I do not have a place to vomit it out. Well, I do but it's not the same and I can only do so much alone when in the presence of God. So, I find myself looking at Facebook groups and seeing everyone's results from different states in the U.S. saying that they received a passing score for the NCE exam. It is important that I remain true to myself and not what others are doing. This will only confuse things. I'm getting discouraged but I keep looking at them. It's hard to but I am which is helping me retain the material. At times I wanted to stop together but I didn't. I am is still discouraged, and it has only been almost two weeks since I took the exam. I am registering for the fall administration. I still feel discouraged and do not think I'll ever pass because I'm getting further away from it. I am doing the best I can and hope it's enough, in Jesus's name.

RE-ROUTING:
THE PERSONAL DISCOVERY OF HOME

"As long as I am still living and breathing, I still have a chance at anything I want in life."

-Ereka Howard

I got to remember that all things work together for the good of them that love the Lord and are called by his purpose. It might not feel like it, but it still is. Just believe it and I will accomplish it. There are things inside of me that have not been used in a while. Dig deeper within me and stay focused on the power that I've always had.

As I am watching a series on tv that is talking about the heritage of Cuba, I cannot help but become more excited about my first trip that is soon to come. I hope that my grandmother will be able to travel with me.

Looking at the restaurants, and homes in Cuba, makes me wonder what my life would have been like if my mother had decided not to come to the U.S. with my grandmother. The show on television talks about the heritage of Cubans. The video mentioned the fact that there is no internet in Cuba, just yet. This documentary was filmed in 2015 so things have changed. For me to communicate with my family in Cuba, it had to be planned ahead of time so that they could get to a Wi-Fi spot. Due to the lack of internet connections, some Cubans are required to go to certain areas of the country to communicate with people in the United States of America. It takes at least 5 days to plan a meeting either over the phone or through video just to communicate with my grandmother, aunt, and or my aunt's friend in Cuba. Communication with my aunt is usually done through people that are members of her church. Since she is not able to communicate with us consistently, she needs additional help. Each time I speak with her through video, the connection is always weak, and it looks like she is in a park or something in Cuba. Out conversations are important and mean a lot to me which explains the frustration that I have when the signal gets weak and this is very frustrating to me. The internet in Cuba is horrible!

Today my Abuelita received her new passport and she opened it while on the phone with me. She was so happy and so was I. It feels like my dream as a child is finally coming together. I am super nervous and excited at the same time. I had to be careful to not stand out while in Cuba as it relates to my clothing... Instead of wearing name-brand clothes, I chose to shop at thrift stores, not only for my wardrobe but for my family in Cuba. About every shirt I saw had something that represented the USA.

I thought to myself, "Maybe my family in Cuba can use this."

While at the thrift store, I bought things that I knew were not available in Cuba, such as fans that produce water while blowing, kitchen mats, towels, socks, undergarments, etc. I set aside a certain amount of money just for my family in Cuba.

RE-ROUTING PT II:
THE PERSONAL DISCOVERY OF HOME

In less than a week, I will be in Cuba with my grandmother for a week. I just texted my mother that I am going to Cuba which was one of the hardest things I have had to do. I did not want to text her because I didn't want to hurt her feelings.

I hesitated to send the text. I erased message after message trying to figure out how to say it. Nervousness set

"Sometimes when adoptees set out to find their biological families, the adoptive family will somehow feel a certain way about everything. To reassure her about what was happening, I told her that I loved her and that nothing will ever change that."

-Ereka Howard

in. It took me a long time to send it, but I finally did. Finally, instead of saying it normally, I just sent a text with the word Cuba with an angel emoji. So, there it is, she knows. If I know anything about her, she will not talk to me for a long time. She will ignore me as she has done several times in the past. I had to text her so I could feel free to go on my trip. My stomach is in knots wondering what she is thinking and how she feels. Ugh! I am going to the gym. Bye.

I spoke with a family member about my trip. She listened to my story and was concerned about my well-being. She had her views and I listened to them. I understood her concern. I just did not want to hurt her feelings. I am not in control of that. The conversation went well, and we talked about other things. She seemed okay with it. This is a huge relief! She knows I am going with my grandmother. I told her the entire story. I do not want to hide anymore. I want to be free to talk about my story to millions around the world. It will happen one day.

I contacted Southwest Airlines today to make sure we had everything ready for our trip. Every day my trip to Cuba got closer— my level of excitement rose. I could hardly believe it when the day arrived! I remember fantasizing about what it would be like to live or be in Cuba. I would search several websites and Google the word "Cuban" to see what they look like and how they act. Now I will be able to see it for myself.

People ask me every day, "Am I ready? Have a safe trip. 'Enjoy My trip." I always reply with, "I will. Thank you."

But deep down inside I am nervous as heck. I don't know what to expect. I feel like a fly trapped inside a car. Well, forget about the trapped part. Let's just say, I feel like I will be the only one there, alone. I know my grandmother is going so that's a relief. I can't believe I was going to make this trip alone. I am running on 41/2 hours of sleep. Making sure that both my bags and bag were clear, was a little rough but we made it through...

Well, Abuelita and I made it and we're off to Cuba. I didn't think we would pass through customs for some reason or another, but we did thank goodness. The lady at check-in almost got us though. Somehow the passports and names didn't add up due to a typo on both identifications.

Before I got frustrated, I took a deep breath, and before I could exhale, the lady said, That's okay, I'm okay."

What a release it was to know that we had everything we needed. So off we go with 20 minutes to make it to our terminal before takeoff.

I told Abuelita, "Rapido!"

The lady kept us at the terminal longer than expected. I grabbed Abuelita's hand and started to speed walk. Looking at Abuelita, I could tell she was getting tired and I was worried not only about missing our flight, but my grandmother's health. She has asthma. That's nothing to play with. As we were speed walking, I looked around for the place where I and my grandmother first met. I can still remember that day. I was on my way back home and had one overlay at the same airport. I was so determined and focused on making our flight, that I didn't even see who was in front of me. I started to speed walk and kept looking back at my grandmother. I was hoping that I could at least get to the terminal and make them wait for my grandmother. They would have no choice but to wait. I couldn't walk in front of her any longer, so I slowed down and grabbed her arm, thinking that the terminal would not be that far. Little did I know that our terminal was back in the corner at the end of the airport. In the words of my Abuelita, "Aye dios mio!" We made it to the terminal and as we were walking, the lady said my name on the intercom. I felt relieved to know that they would remind me. I walked to the counter and gave my boarding pass to the lady. I went to my grandmother and asked for hers, but she couldn't find it. I was like, "Really?" I looked and looked for it again but could not find the one for the first flight.

Looking at us scramble through our items, the lady said, "That's okay. You're good." Go us Woo-hoo! We finally make it to the door of the plane, and I explain to her our flight itinerary.

She said, "Okay Mamacita es okay mama."

I love to hear those words. There were literally no seats inside the plane. I was worried about splitting up from my grandmother. Luckily, we found two seats sort of close to each other in the very front of the plane.

I asked a lady if my grandmother could sit there, and she said "Yes."

Abuelita was in front of me looking for a seat.

"Abuelita!" I quietly yelled, "Aqui esta bien."

The lady said, "It's ok. I speak Spanish."

I found a seat two rows behind her on the other side of the plane in eyesight. We were both seated and safe. On the plane next to me was a man who was originally from Cuba but worked between Florida and Texas. He moved away when he was one year old. We talked for several minutes. The man educated me on how Cubans migrated to the USA years ago. I told him my grandmother was one of those. I learned a lot of things I didn't know beforehand about Cuba. He also told me about how difficult life was when all the hurricanes hit about a month ago back-to-back in Cuba, Florida, and other areas. The gentleman explained that he was asked to evacuate suddenly along with family members. His rental car got damaged during the evacuation, but luckily, he had insurance. I believe he got back home from Florida to Texas or was it vice versa? I'm not entirely sure, but he said he got back home with 10 miles left in the gas tank. Due to my friendly behavior, meeting new people has never been an issue for me. The conversation lasted over 25 minutes until we took off. The man was a good person and I'm glad we exchanged conversation.

We're in Tampa waiting on other passengers to board. We stayed on the same flight. While waiting on other passengers, I got a chance to talk with the flight crew and tell them my story. Come to find out, the captain was adopted also. He told the flight crew and us his story. Talk about wow! Okay bye. Gotta go. Here we come Ft. Lauderdale! While on the flight we met yet another Cuban lady who moved from Cuba in the '70s also. I asked her when was the last time she was in Cuba.

She said, "When I first left, I'm afraid to go back."

I wanted to take a photo with her I decided not to. She and my grandmother had the greatest conversation. They talked about when they both left Cuba and why they left their families in Cuba, how hard their lives have been, and how they are now since leaving. Both of them had h good and bad experiences regarding government findings. They were communicating in the Cuban language. They didn't know each other; they just happen to meet each other on the flight. This trip is already turning out to be amazing. All I hear are stories about how Cubans left for better lives. So many Cubans in America decided to never go back. The other lady was so sweet. Remember all the nights I and My family talked together at the table until 2-3 a.m.? I was joking about bringing my cousin to America. to America in My suitcase? This is a reminder I had to have to get ready for what was getting ready to happen. I showed My family how I would do it. I also told them that I favor My cousin Toledo. Everyone thought so also. I, My aunt, and Luisa all have the same personality. Remember when I and My cousins walked together to drop off My cousin Luis at the bus stop? They held My hand and made sure I was always safe. The guys had so many laughs together. Remember when I and My cousin would sit outside and talk about how things were in Cuba? The talks I guys had about how much he loved me and want me to be safe. Remember sitting on the steps in front of the hotel? Remember the many times y'all walked to the game room to buy water and other drinks? The first time I tasted soda from Cuba and water as well? Remember when My aunt woke me up to tell me to come to eat after taking a nap on Sunday evening? Remember her waking me up on Sunday morning when everyone in the house was snoring while sleeping? She rubbed/ actuated My foot to wake me up. I woke up slowly. Everything regarding this trip was pre-orchestrated for me before I was born. This includes the people, experiences, and even food that I experienced while in Cuba. From the check-in personnel in the airports and people we met in Cuba, everything and everyone was pre-orchestrated to see and meet me for a reason at the right and perfect time. I know where I came from. This is not the last trip.

The first time I saw a photo of my mother was when Abuelita asked me to come downstairs when I was putting on makeup and getting ready for the day? My grandmother showed me another photo of My bio mom in 1986. It was a color photo. She then took me to the kitchen where the family album was. It was a whole album of the whole family tree. The night before, I was so scared while being in the hotel and getting ready for bed. I kept seeing things in the bathroom and it felt like someone was always behind me. I ran downstairs and could not fall asleep. I had not felt anything like that since being in Cuba. It felt like I was being followed and I saw stuff. It was probably My mother's spirit. I didn't know the next morning I was going to see another photograph of her the next day along with other photos of my family in Cuba. Two nights before, I felt a peaceful spirit when I and the family were walking at night.

I was going to write about how we went to El Malecon in Cuba, but I can't. My stomach is literally in knots, and I had to be given medicine. It has not hurt like this in years so goodnight. It was fun today and very productive because I got other photos of my mom and family in Cuba. Remember the last day I am in Cuba before going back to America? Remember how hard it was to communicate with My family? It was tough, very tough. As I was reflecting on what happened the day before, I kept replaying everything in my mind.

I asked questions like: "Why don't the police help?"

They were just looking at us while changing the time. It was at least ten total plus everyone in the street and other cars passing. Some taxicab drivers in Cuba don't use the same tools. Remember what tools he used to fix the time? It was not the same jack. I was with both of My little cousins. Remember how everything was and how I felt? What did I see and how did it feel to see him struggling? It was an old car also just like others. Remember what I smelled and what I saw? Y'all had to leave him and get in another taxi. Once his car was sort of fixed, y'all got in the car and headed to My original destination.

What is their lifestyle like and what did I experience while in Cuba? What did I see? What was the transportation etc. like? What did they drive? Trackers, etc.? Yes! Look at all the videos and photos I took. What did the neighborhoods and homes/ rooms look like? The different cities in Cuba?

Returning to Cuba: Well, I'm leaving Cuba in less than one hour. It's a bittersweet but hard pill to swallow. I could tell that it was hard for My family to let me and granny go. My cousins cried, with my cousin crying the most. Knowing how hard they have it in Cuba and the lifestyle, I wanted to take them with I. Deep down inside, I wanted to cry, but couldn't because I knew everyone would cry just by the thought of thinking about My mom.

It was difficult for me to communicate with my family especially in the time of an emergency, not to mention when I got really sick and almost had to go to the hospital in Cuba. How funny it was to my family to mention the word "Coco" coconut. It was the fruit or other food that I ate that had me sick throughout the night with only getting 3-4 hours of sleep. My entire family wanted me to go to the beach which was two minutes away from the place where y'all stayed. My stomach was hurting bad. It took over two to three hours to get myself together... I didn't get any sleep the night before. For the next 3 days, I was extremely careful about what I ate. Also, when I could not use My phone a lot or when I could not use my credit card. I had to call family in America to send money to Western Union. It was hard receiving the money and it had to be changed 3 times with the last having to be my cousin's name. Americans could not receive money. Also, remember all the walking I did? Are the many busy rides full of Cubans? Yay! my cousins/family stood by my side the entire time. Things moved so fast and quickly, that I couldn't even grasp being in Cuba half of the time but it's okay. I made the best of it. From the many walks and dancing, eating the same food night and day. Going to the store to buy "Fresca" or "Pan/ Ban" (bread), all the noises and smells of good ol' Cuba... To the many stories about My mother and her friends in Cuba/ family. For the first time getting another picture of her to hearing stories and seeing people who look exactly like me. It was a great trip and a good experience. From the cold/ warm showers to living the actual Cuban lifestyle with My family. It was an adjustment and taught me to appreciate being American. It's hard leaving My family in Cuba. I am sitting on the plane writing notes about My experience and the visuals/ experiences in Cuba. Don't take America for granted. There were no nail shops, no massage shops, etc. in Cuba whatsoever! Cubans don't have the same luxury as Americans. I and Abuelita left pieces of y'all in Cuba like the neck rests and my special orange blanket. Remember the items y'all gave to My family from America: Food, jewelry, bags, medicine, etc.? I can now say that I've lived on an island and in another country while being with family. I lived the Cuban lifestyle. I did what I had to do to survive each day while trying to make sure My grandmother was safe at the same time. Remember the weather and how hot it was each day?

With reflection about my trip I told myself, Remember how much I wanted to come to Cuba a week ago? Well, now I can say I've been to and met my biological family in Cuba. Now I know how it feels to be my grandmother while in America. It's hard to communicate in a country that does not speak the same language as I do. It's a very secretive country that's owned by the government. Remember how I felt just being around My blood family and with My biological grandmother? I fulfilled My childhood dream. Don't forget where I came from and how to appreciate the life I have lived.

Let this experience inspire me to exceed My expectations in life. Once in a lifetime experience. They can't just leave freely like Americans. They must be cleared by the government to leave the island of Cuba. The money differences etc. I didn't eat American food on purpose for one week. I had no choice. The First American food returning from Cuba was the pretzels and peanuts while on the flight, lol. It was Abuelita's first time flying.

Not too many people can say they've been to Cuba... I missed America but wanted to experience Cuba as much as possible. I wanted to learn a lesson. Ereka, keep pushing and moving forward, at least for My family in Cuba.

Honestly, I didn't realize how hard it was to live in Cuba. Not saying I didn't appreciate the life I live but it made me appreciate it more. The very first big food item I ate in the airport was a Chex mix. I swear it tasted like a baked potato and steak, lol. Man, me and

Abuelita tore those snacks up. We were starving and forgot how American food tasted. Remember the joke My primo said about My other prima being from Angola? Also, is everyone being Angola? it was so funny! After getting off the flight, I felt like I heard the noises of Cuba even though I was not in Cuba anymore. It was embedded inside My soul and spirit and always will be. I was so nervous in the beginning, not knowing how the trip would turn out. I thought I would not be accepted or be able to connect or communicate with My family. That was a lie from hell and was a trick of the enemy. I act just like My aunt and have the same personality as her and my other cousins Luisita, Luis, Yoel, and many others. I also felt connected to other Cubans and their lifestyle. I am Cuban. Remember going out to eat and noticing every food item I ate that was American.

The day after returning from Cuba, I woke up the next morning feeling like I were still in Cuba. Guess this is what they call "Jetlag." I drive My car for the first time, and it also felt weird, lol. Everything felt weird and different while being back in America. I didn't see everything the same as I always did before traveling to Cuba. Everything was a big tradition. It was hard for me to wake up the next morning because I was stuck in the time zone Everything regarding this trip was predestined and planned just for me, my biological mother was with me the whole time.

She was so excited to see me and know that I made it back safely. She asked questions about My trip and wanted to see photos. While explaining the experience, I was careful with what I was saying because I didn't want to hurt her feelings. I was trying to ignore the fact that she wanted to see photos from the trip. Finally, she asked again, and I decided to show her. She first saw a photo of not only My Abuelita but the family in Cuba. She took it well and appeared to not have a problem with seeing the photos of the family, this makes me feel more comfortable. It was tough but I did it. It was a great visit. All of My family asked how My trip went. This trip was more than a vacation or trip to Cuba, it was confirmation and set me free in so many ways. I am thankful for the opportunity. Not too many can say the same. Remember telling My family how much I was going to tell My story to the world when I got back to America? I also decided to make the trip to Cuba around the most crucial time when President Trump was in the process of stopping travel to and from Cuba. I went just a few weeks after 3-4 hurricanes occurred and struck Cuba and the other islands around, not to mention Hurricane Irma. I stayed in one of the residential areas that were severely affected by the storm as well. While walking to the bus stops on some days, I saw several homes and businesses that were destroyed, trees in the street, homes destroyed, windows busted, etc. But I made the trip, even after it was postponed due to Abuelita's passport not being finalized. Now that was a process! On the first day, the guys were supposed to stay somewhere preplanned by me through Airbnb but had to change at the last minute due to Abuelita's health. It took one-three hours to finally find somewhere to stay while in Cuba. However, it all worked out, I and Abuelita paid for a loaded house right off La playa, and come to find out it was a resort. It wasn't cheap, but worth it. Waking up with My family every day and night eating and sleeping under one roof was the best time ever and what seemed to be a problem, ended up being a solution.

Back in America. Praise Jesus I am connected to the world again. Cut off from humanity, I loved it all very much. God bless and thanks for sharing my first experience to reunite with my family in Cuba. Oh boy, do I have another story to tell? Remember trying to help My family in Cuba and the promise I made to Myself when I left and headed back to America? Almost immediately I sent money for food etc. not sure what they would do with it. I trusted God and will continue to do so. I also am planning on sending them items from America (food, clothes, etc.) I love and appreciate My family in Cuba. I also sent My cousin a text message asking him to pray and set up a specific time to pray together while he is in Cuba and I are in America. He has not responded yet. I might have to send him money again. It's okay. Remember when you consistently sent money to My family and had to quit is the questions I asked myself. I felt horrible because I didn't want them to depend on me all the time. What if I can't help them literally and they begin to become dependent? It's going to hurt me rather than help me. Everything I saw and experienced while in Cuba should inspire me and want better out of life. It will. Make it Ereka! Don't look back either no matter what or who tries to stop me. I got this and God's got me. The way we imagine other countries to be is insane. As a child before reuniting with my biological family, I had dreams to meet my family in Cuba. I didn't know how or when; I just knew it was going to happen! More than 3 decades later, that vision came true. Life is something we should never take for granted. On the other side of the world, others are fighting day after day living off of what they can barely receive. Don't take things or people for granted. I am going to have battles and struggles in life. Most of them occur because of our perspectives. Shut up and sit down!

"This is something that I have to tell myself every so often just to be able to silence the negative thoughts inside of my head."

-Ereka Howard

Now, I know you're completely confused as to who I am talking to throughout this entire book? Since I was a child, I can remember encouraging myself to get through the tough times in my life or at least what was going on inside of my head. To continue on this voyage, I want to let you in on my alter ego. Some of you have not been able to get to know the intellectual Ereka and now is the time to let her out and be able to shine. Since you have been able to read about my story, now I want to introduce tactical information and research done regarding some of the difficulties that I have encountered throughout my life. So sit back, continue reading and take notes as I invite you into the research portion of my book. The next section of this book consists of the research that I did as it relates to my life. Enjoy!

RE-ROUTING MY JOURNEY:
THE HOW-TO

Stop complaining and start fighting! Things and people will not be given to us on a silver plate! Stay focused and consistent on those dreams.

-Ereka Howard

Adoption is a topic that is near and dear to my heart. When coming into the program at The University of North Texas at Dallas, I mentioned in my interview that I wanted to become a counselor so that I would be able to help those who are struggling with mental illness as it relates to adoption. Throughout this program, my focus has been on adoption. Not knowing that there was more to adoption than just a child being adopted, I automatically assumed that my story was the only story out there.

Adoption, as a topic, has been researched both quantitatively and qualitatively. It is not only about abuse, but there are studies associated with why a child might become adopted. Transracial adoptions continue to happen to children all over the world. Many children have been adopted but never met their biological families. Some dream about that one day when they will be able to meet the family that they look like. When adopted children meet their families, mental illnesses can either improve or get worse. Adopted children grow up with traumatic experiences that they carry on into adulthood. Some can handle the pressures of being adopted, while others either end up homeless, incarcerated, or hospitalized. Some children grow up to become successful beings that give back to the community. Research in this area has been a supporting factor while trying to find out why this population struggles with mental illness. Not only workers, and teachers, but genetics and the environment can determine how the adoptee will live my life. Adoption is different from "fostering." Adoption and fostering can be the same thing biologically while they can be different. Some children are adopted by the next of kin while others are placed into foster care homes.

On the other hand, some children are not adopted through kinship. Some are adopted internationally or even out of the hospital. It all depends on the adoption agency or state along with many other determining factors. It is important to distinguish between adoption and fostering. The former is indicative of a complete separation of a child from the biological parents; the latter is a situation where a child is placed in a family, but the legal parenting responsibilities are taken over by the state, usually the welfare system (Mahmood, 2015). Adopting a child takes an enormous amount of work, dedication, luck, and money. Regardless of whether it is a domestic or international adoption, there are many hoops to jump through to have custody of a child. Adoption can change a child's life and the parents' lives for the better, but studies have shown this life-changing decision can be risky. Most children who are adopted flourish into mentally and physically healthy individuals. They learn to assimilate themselves into the new surroundings and adjust without many challenges. Greater challenges, such as language and cultural barriers, occur more often with international adoptions than with domestic adoptions.

Children are up for adoption for a multitude of reasons: The parents are deceased, the children were abandoned, or they are wardens of the state due to poor parenting. Babies who are found in dumpsters are alive and are also brought into the foster care system. Mothers addicted to drugs often have their newborns taken away after birth. Overseas, many mothers cannot afford to take care of their children and may be in poor health themselves. Adopted persons often lack both family genetic and medical history. This information can be vitally important to the diagnosis and treatment of genetically based medical conditions. In addition, being asked to supply medical history information at a doctor's appointment may make adopted persons acutely aware of how they differ from those who were not adopted. Finding out later in life that they were adopted as infants put adopted persons at risk of misdiagnoses or other medical issues due to the long-held assumption of a family medical history that they later find to be incorrect. Additionally, when adopted persons plan to get married or become a parent, they may want to know about genetic characteristics that the children may inherit.

In many cases, non-identifying information, such as medical history, may be placed in the adoption file by the birth parents or agency at the time of the adoption. Adopted persons are allowed access to this non-identifying information, which is usually at least as old as the adopted person. In some States, adopted persons can petition a judge to have the adoption records opened. Judges will agree to do so to provide urgently needed medical information. However, obtaining access to information provided by the birth parents at the time of the adoption may not be sufficient to provide a full medical history. For example, a birth parent, sibling, or grandparent may later develop or be diagnosed with a genetic disease or condition. It is more useful if both parents regularly update the file that is kept with the adoption agency or attorney. Additionally, those in open adoptions may be able to get this information directly from the birth parents (Child Welfare Information Gateway).

Based on my research, in the United States, approximately 120,000 children are adopted annually, and adopted individuals constitute about 1.5 million children younger than the age of 18 years. Things are changing, however, as a decreasing number of domestic adoptions has been accompanied by a sharp increase in the number of international adoptions. Did you know that over 40,000 children per year are moved between more than 100 countries through adoption? I found out that despite the popularity of adoption, there is a persistent concern that adopted children may be at heightened risk for mental health or adjustment problems. Previous research has shown that adopted children with a history of prenatal substance exposure or pre-placement deprivation and those who were placed relatively late in the adoptive homes are at heightened risk of social, intellectual, and emotional problems. Nonetheless, existing research has not resolved the extent to which those adoptees with a good pre-placement history and an early age at the placement are at increased risk for clinically relevant mental health problems. A child may initially enjoy the warmth and comfort of being" chosen" but gradually develop an awareness of having been adopted, bringing with it the possibility of uncertainty and several unanswered questions. School can be an unhappy place for these children, as they are often confronted with questions they cannot or do not know how to answer; this is particularly the case when teachers give lessons that focus on family roots. This includes doing projects that require the adoptee to try to figure out where they come from. Some adoptees know nothing about their families and their whereabouts. This can be a trigger for the adoptee which in return, can cause a mental breakdown and discomfort. Being adopted can be a traumatic event and should be regarded as such in the life of the child. The loss of the birth parents as a result of adoption sets the stage for the feelings of loss and abandonment that many adopted persons experience at some point in their lives (Mahmood, 2015).

"The construct of race is distinct from ethnicity in its emphasis on *power* relations. A set of historically and socially derived practices, race is imposed by those in power (Whites)to sort people into groups according to perceived physical and behavioral characteristics" (Chang, 2017, p. 309). These socially constructed categories assign differential value, power, and privilege to groups, thus establishing a social status hierarchy used to justify the exploitation, dehumanization, and oppression of non-Whites (Markus, 2008). As such, racial socialization by white adoptive parents necessarily means acknowledging the existence of such a hierarchy that would rank the children below their parents, thus requiring that those children learn to cope with systemic forms of racial bias and oppression from which the white parents are exempt. Given the inherent violence in the construct of race, and the guilt often elicited by the unearned privileges that accompany whiteness, it is not surprising that white parents typically avoid discussing race with their children (Chang, 2017).

These childhood sufferings of a pure psychic order are slow and persistent, and they have never been recognized as potential causes of psychic illness in adults. Attachment Theory is said to be a stable theory to use with those who are adopted. "For the adoptee, the experience of loss is usually felt in the context of the search for self" (Brodzinsky, 1992, p. 12). Attachment theory helps those who deal with attachment disorder regulate their feelings and emotions. Since most adoptees suffer from this disorder, utilizing this theory will contribute to their overall well-being positively. The use of attachment theory within adoption will help the adoptee securely function in a positive way where they will be able to manage strong, powerful feelings positively and healthily.

Adopted children may feel guilt and blame themselves for the adoption, which can also lead to low self-esteem, and the resulting behavior may be a key indicator of how frightened they are feeling inside (Mahmood, 2015). Feeling guilty or blaming themselves for being adopted can cause the adoptee to have distorted thoughts about their lives. Adopted children struggling with learning problems are significantly larger than non-adopted children. Often, adolescents can also struggle mentally and emotionally. Identity is also an important thing as the child begins to mature. Once the child begins to develop, he or she will wonder what the parents or other family members look like.

The task of adopted adolescents' identity development is often more difficult and includes questions about the biological family, why he or she was placed for adoption, what became of the birth parents, whether the adolescent resembles the birth parents in looks or other characteristics, and where the adolescent 'belongs' in terms of education, social class, culture, peer group, and more. Often, adoptees wonder why they were adopted. As stated previously in this research paper, adoptees will begin to feel guilty or shameful for being adopted. For example, the adoptee will think that the biological parents did not want them because of the way they looked or acted. As the child gets older and develops in the environment, he or she will either adapt or break away from the environment. The environment can be the main reason why they were placed up for adoption or put into a foster home.

This often contributes to adolescents' lives negatively, and in return, the adolescent will begin to act out negatively. The adopted children wondered why they were placed for adoption or what was "wrong" with them that caused the birth parents to give them up. This reveals the predicament in which an adopted child may be placed. When children feel they do not belong and are not significant they often develop defensive or "survival" behavior, which is often perceived as challenging (Mahmood, 2015, p. 28). However, the term "adoption-competent" has lacked a standardized, broadly accepted definition (Atkinson, 2013). Although the terms "adoption-competent" and "adoption sensitive" are frequently used in professional literature and research, the terms have lacked standardized, well-accepted definitions. It appears that adoptive families readily recognize adoption competent practices (or the absence of such practices) but that information about the nature of specific practices that would be deemed adoption competent remains scant. The absence of a standardized definition of adoption competency and the formal specification of knowledge, skills, and values associated with adoption competency have hampered the study of adoption competency and the systematic development of adoption competencies in services providers (Atkinson, 2013, p. 157).

Participant comments further illuminate the nature of practice changes. Those who reported that training had influenced information collected at intake and during initial assessment reported they were collecting more background information, were more aware of adoption issues, were using new assessment questions and procedures, and were more comfortable asking adoption questions (Atkinson, 2013). Training participants whose clinical approaches were influenced by training report a greater understanding of evidence-based approaches, placing greater emphasis on loss and grief and the use of new tools (Atkinson,

2013). Fifty-eight percent of respondents report changes in practices at the organizational level such as strengthened intake protocols, adding parent and support/education groups to services offered, and creation of post-adoption specialist positions within agencies. Training is an important factor while trying to help adoptees. Adoptees need to know that the person who is trying to help them, really cares about them. Not only is it hard for adoptees to develop trust, but it is also hard for them to understand what it takes to become better people while working through their mental illnesses (Atkinson, 2013). Ongoing training is needed, and it helps the therapist and/ or staff become competent in the mental illnesses and perspectives of those who are adopted.

The following within this research shows how effective they are within kinship competency. This means that 485 persons responded to the survey of which 87% were adoptive parents, 9.1% were adopted persons, 8.1% were members of an adoptive family, 7% were birth parents, and 17.2% reported themselves in an "other" role, typically a professional role related to adoption. Respondents were allowed to select more than one role and 37% reported more than one role. The extent to which those who responded have multiple connections to adoption is noteworthy. About 16% of the 419 adoptive parents who responded reported working in a related professional capacity such as social Adoption Competent Clinical Practice 167 workers, therapists, attorneys/advocates, or foster parents. Similarly, of the 44 adopted persons responding, 21 (or 48%) reported being adoptive parents and 24% reported additional adoption-related roles, including social worker, therapist, foster parent, and special educator. Persons responding were from 40 states and seven countries outside the United States (Atkinson, 2013). Here are some considerations to think about. The potential adoptee's unique needs also should be considered. Is the child physically handicapped or mentally challenged, and is my patient capable of handling these issues? Would there be a good temperament fit between the potential adoptive parent and child? Because child adoption laws vary from state to state, there are no established criteria for determining the eligibility of an individual with a history of mental illness.

The success of child adoption by an individual with a history of mental illness will depend on state laws and the policy of the adoption agency. Some U.S. states and territories (Alaska, Arizona, California, Kentucky, North Dakota, and Puerto Rico) regard parental mental illness as aggravated circumstances. The loss of both parents because of adoption may set the stage for feelings of grief for many adopted persons. The loss experienced by adopted persons may be characterized as ambiguous loss or the loss of someone who still is (or who may be) alive. This type of loss also may increase the feelings of uncertainty an adopted person feels. Adopted persons who feel secure in the adoption and have open adoptive family communication may be better able to manage the uncertainty and grief. Additionally, adopted persons may have difficulty finding an outlet because the grief may not be recognized by others. Feelings of loss and grief, as well as anger, anxiety, or fear, may especially occur during emotionally charged milestones, such as marriage, the birth of a child, or the death of a parent.

Adopted persons may also suffer secondary losses. For instance, along with the loss of the birth mother and birth father, adopted persons may experience the loss of brothers and sisters, grandparents, aunts and uncles, and cousins. There also may be a loss of cultural connection or language (in cases of intercountry or transracial adoption). For those who were adopted as older children, there may be a loss of friends, foster families, pets, schools, and neighborhoods (Child Welfare Information Gateway). Mental Health professionals that constantly work with adopted children are not aware of the problems associated with adoption. Some adoptees do not would rather not talk to mental health professionals because they do not feel comfortable. The following percentages mentioned will give a better understanding of how this affects this population. About 81% of respondents reported they had seen one or more mental health professionals or been involved with the treatment of another family member. Eighty-four percent of adoptive parents and 77% of adopted persons reported having seen a mental health professional. Of the 382 respondents who reported they had seen a mental health professional, 24.87% reported that the mental health professionals were adoption-competent, 26.18% reported the mental health professionals were not adoption-competent, and 48.95% reported that some were, and some were not adoption-competent. Of the 346 adoptive parents who reported seeing a mental health professional, 26.88% responded that the mental health professional was adoption competent, 23.99% responded that the person was not adoption-competent, and 49.13% responded that "some were, and some weren't," suggesting a slightly better experience than the group (Atkinson, 2013, p. 168). "Good casework prepares parent and children, decreasing the rates of disruption and dissolution" (Gray, 2007, p. 200). A home study should be an educational opportunity for parents to keep them within their capacity for successful parenting. A social worker's job is to facilitate the formation of close relationships through families. While some families who want to adopt and are willing to assist with the development processes of children in need of a family, it is important to continue to view these families as working units (Gray, 2007). The placement field has suffered after taking a stance that all children can and should be placed into family holes.

The Adoption and Safe Families Act of 1997 (ASFA) requires that child welfare agencies find permanent families for children who cannot return to their birth parents. The number of children adopted from foster care has significantly increased since the enactment of ASFA. While most adoptions succeed, 10 to 25 percent disrupt before finalization and a smaller percentage dissolve after finalization. There has been a growing recognition that adoptive families need services to help them address the children's mental health issues and other problems. Post-adoption services are particularly critical for families whose adopted children have disabilities because these adoptions are at the greatest risk of disruption. ASFA's promise of permanence for children in foster care will not be realized unless adoptive families have the support they need to stay together. Adoption has played a prominent role in federal child welfare law and practice, from the 1980 passage of the Adoption Assistance and Child Welfare Act through the enactment of ASFA in 1997 (North American Council on Adoptable Children, 2007). Adjusting to an environment is often a challenge for adoptees who are older than 10 years old. Depending on where the adoptee came from and the demographics, he or she will struggle with adjusting to a specific environment. The adjustment of adoptees tends to be positive, and placements are quite secure with relatively low rates of dissolution, particularly for children adopted as infants (Agnich, 2016). However, studies of the well-being of adoptees need to account for openness, that is, whether the adoptive parents and/or child continue contact with the birth family after the adoption. Open adoptions are complicated because several factors can influence openness, such as the child's history of abuse and neglect, the comfort level of adoptive parents, and access to support services, all of which can also impact the child's well-being (Agnich, 2016). "Therapeutic interventions for the poorly attached child need to draw upon cognitive behavioral techniques to help the child to access these various parts of self as he develops from the past through the present to the future" (Hughes, 2004, p. 73). The majority of adopted children are emotionally and behaviorally healthy; however, a small minority is vulnerable to adjustment issues and disproportionately receives mental health treatment. Specifically, adopted children are more likely than non-adoptees to have attachment disorders, depression, conduct disorders, and externalizing behavior problems, (i.e., drug use, physical aggressiveness, antisocial behaviors, etc.). Exposure to childhood trauma, such as physical and sexual abuse, neglect, family and community violence, placement instability, and institutionalized care, can also lead to an increased risk of attachment difficulties and posttraumatic stress disorder. Thus, adoptees with early adversities have a higher risk for these and other psychiatric disorders (Agnich, 2016). For the sessions to be fully therapeutic, focusing on both the pain and hope along with the problems will increase the positive outcomes of each session. Availability of information, in large part due to the Internet, adopted persons now have access to widespread information and resources, which can greatly aid them in discovering information about their birth families or finding resources for support and encouragement (Child Welfare Information).

Adopted persons generally lead lives that are very similar to their non-adopted peers, but the adoption experience frequently can contribute to circumstances that the adopted person may need to overcome, such as feelings of loss and grief, questions about self-identity, or a lack of information about the medical background. The increasing occurrence of open adoption— and therefore the increased contact adopted persons have with their birth families— has dramatically affected the issues faced by adopted persons over the past two decades. Whereas adopted persons from a past era may have more frequently dealt with issues of secrecy and large information gaps, persons adopted recently may more often be faced with issues related to having contact with the birth parents. Every day adopted children are suffering from a mental illness that began happening as a child. Some children will suffer from a mental illness due to genetics or the environment they live in or were raised in. The need for current research is required to help children become successful while having a mental illness. In many cases, it is also linked to experiences of early life adversity. The following things are reasons that can cause mental illnesses in adoptees. Prenatal exposure to drugs and alcohol, neglect, abuse, multiple foster placements, and orphanage life can contribute to mental illnesses. Both the normative and traumatic experiences commonly associated with being adopted create emotional complexities for adopted individuals and increased parenting challenges for the families often resulting in the need for mental health services. Adoptees w also struggle with identity throughout life. One way for the adoptive parents to contribute to their lives positively is that the parents welcome and accept the adoptee for who they are, including their ethnicity and background. Depending on the age of the adoptee, he or she will go through different processes while trying to find out who they are.

Specific adoption-related problems identified included: feelings of rejection by the birthmother; anger toward birth and/or adoptive parents; using the adoptive status for revenge or to hurt adoptive parents; and rootlessness, self-hatred, and/or resentment about being adopted. One factor that is generally considered to lead to these problems is difficulties in managing normative adoption-related issues in the family, such as creating open and empathic parent-child communication about adoption, sharing adoption information with the child, supporting the child's curiosity about his/her origins, maintaining respect for the child's birth family and culture, helping the child integrate being adopted into the emerging identity, and, when appropriate, supporting the child's need for contact with birth family (Brodzinsky, 2016).

"Neglected children suffer hurts in the bodies, minds, emotions, and spirits" (Monteleon, 1998, p. 68). Children who are dealing with neglect will suffer from life-long problems throughout their lives. Once the child becomes older, he or she will continue to deal with neglect. For example, if something happens in the relationship and the other person leaves them, the adopted person will feel neglected or abandoned if the issue is not fixed early on in life. These family-based problems, which can impact children's character structure, identity, self-esteem, and parent-child relationships, are often contributing factors in the referral of adopted for both outpatient mental health services and residential treatment services. Another set of factors is pre-adoption adversities, such as toxic prenatal environments, early maltreatment, multiple caregivers, and orphanage life (Brodzinsky, 2016). One of the most frequent complaints from adoptive families is the inability to find mental health care from professionals who have both clinical and adoption competence. Competency in adoption is v important for those wanting to work with children and adults who have been adopted. T Research is lacking in this area and there are very few items available as it relates to staff competencies within adoption. "Adopted children, however, were found to exhibit higher levels of externalizing symptoms (attentional difficulties, oppositional tendencies, defiant and conduct problems, and learning problems) but not internalizing disorders (depression, anxiety, and thought disorders" (Wiley, 2017, p. 986). This does not justify everything that adoptees struggle with. Although the research states that adoptees do not struggle with internal difficulties, it is apparent that they do. Some adoptees struggle with internalized and externalized illnesses. Depending on the adoptee and where the adoption took place, for example, the genetics and environment say that they will also have difficulties. There has been an increase over the past 10 years toward looking more closely at negative adoption trends and historical patterns that have existed and continue to exist. One of these trends is that of unregulated custody transfer or "private rehoming" of adopted children using social media as an underground market for adopted children (Wiley, 2017). As I can see from the research completed above, there is a definite need for additional training for clinicians and others working in the field of adoption. There has been some progress throughout the years however, clinicians are still struggling with understanding the child or adult who was adopted. Birth families are also struggling with the child they adopted due to not being able to cognitively understand the adoptee and the struggles. Some adoptees dealt with trauma and are not able to remember it while others who were adopted at an older age, can remember every characteristic of the adoption and why it occurred. Some also have negative feelings about their biological families which prevents them from allowing anyone else to help them.

In conclusion, we all go through things in life that can either make or break us. Sometimes we have to become resilient enough to break the stigmas within our belief systems and experiences. This is a hard thing to do if you've never experienced any hardships in life. What you have read is only 30% of my life and there is more to come soon. Always remember that your story is the ending of someone's beginning. Be careful to not identify with the difficulties that happened in your life. Sometimes our crisis is what makes us who we are and there is nothing wrong with that. Embrace the difficult and release the difficult so that you can become successful. What's your identity crisis?

REFERENCES
&
BIBLIOGRAPHY

Agnich, L. E., Schueths, A. M., James, T. D., & Klibert, J. (2016). The effects of adoption openness and type on the mental health, delinquency, and family relationships of adopted Ith. *Sociological Spectrum*, July/Summer *36*(5), 321-336.

Askeland, K. G., Sivertsen, B., Skogen, J. C., La Greca, A. M., Tell, G. S., Aarø, L. E., & Hysing, M. (2018). Alcohol and drug use among internationally adopted adolescents: Results from a

Norwegian population-based study. *American Journal Of Orthopsychiatry*, *88*(2), 226-235.

Atkinson, A. J., Gonet, P. A., Freundlich, M., & Riley, D. B. (2013). Adoption competent clinical practice: Defining its meaning and development. *Adoption Quarterly*, July/Summer *16*(3-4), 156-174.

Barr, T. L., & Carlisle, K. (2003). *Adoption for dummies*. Hoboker, NJ: Wiley.

Brodzinsky, D., Santa, J., & Smith, S. L. (2016). Adopted Ith in residential care: Prevalence rate and Professional training needs. *Residential Treatment For Children & Youth*, April/Spring *33*(2), 118-134.

Brodzinsky, D., Schechter, M. D., & Henig, R. M. (1993). *Being adopted: The lifelong search for self*. New York: Anchor Books.

Chang, D. F., Feldman, K., & Easley, H. (2017). 'I'm learning not to tell I': Korean transracial Adoptees' appraisals of parental racial socialization strategies and perceived effects. *Asian American Journal Of Psychology*, December/Winter *8*(4), 308-322.

Crumbley, J. (1999). *Transracial adoption and foster care: Practice issues for professionals*. Washington, D.C.: CWLA Press.

Dudley, R., & Mapp, S. C. (2016). Effects of cultural gender roles on international adoptees acculturation. *Social Development Issues: Alternative Approaches To Global Human Needs*, January/Winter *38*(3), 51-63.

Gray, D. D. (2012). *Nurturing adoptions: Creating resilience after neglect and trauma*. London: Jessica Kingsley.

Gorbett, D. (2007). *Adopted teens only: A survival guide to adolescence*. Lincoln, NE: IUniverse Star. Hughes, D. A. (2004). *Facilitating developmental attachment*. Lanham, MD: Rowman & Littlefield.

Keyes, M. A., Sharma, A., Elkins, I. J., Iacono, W. G., & McGue, M. (2008). The Mental Health of U.S. Adolescents Adopted in

Infancy. *Archives of Pediatrics & Adolescent Medicine*, May/Spring *162*(5), 419–425.

Mahmood, S., & Visser, J. (2015). Adopted children: A question of identity. *Support For Learning*, September/Fall *30*(3), 268-285.

Malti, T., Noam, G. G., Beelmann, A., & Sommer, S. (2016). Good enough? Interventions for child mental health: From adoption to adaptation—From programs to systems. *Journal Of Clinical Child And Adolescent Psychology*, Nov-Dec/Fall/Winter *45*(6), 707-709.

Monteleone, J. A. (1998). *A parents & teachers handbook on identifying and preventing child abuse*. St. Louis, MO: G.W. Medical Pub. Wiley, M. O. (2017). Adoption research, practice, and societal trends: Ten years of progress. *American Psychologist*, *72*(9), 985-995.

Shailesh Jain, Rakesh Jain, "MD Edge Psychiatry." Accessed June 21, 2021.

https://www.mdedge.com/psychiatry/article/76413/practice-management/adoption-mentally-ill-individuals what-recommend.

ACKNOWLEDGEMENTS

I would like to acknowledge the extraordinary debt I owe to God, my family, spiritual parents, friends, and mentors. You guys are the bomb.com! Also, thank you BOBM Publishing for being patient with my perfectionism lol. Also, thank you to all the mental health professionals nationwide who continue to sacrifice your services. Adoptees nationwide, continue to use your voice! To my professors and mentors, thank you for holding me accountable and last, but definitely not least, thank you my emotional support animal Serenity who allowed me to finish this book when she wanted to play. I want to mention that I do not think I would be alive if it was not for all the ministries that pray for me. Thank you everyone!

This is just the beginning...

ABOUT
THE
AUTHOR

Ms. Ereka Howard is no one-dimensional sensation.

She is a speaker, co-author, Certified Life Coach, Clinician, and Adoptee. Since the precocious age of eight, Ms. Ereka Howard has graced and impacted audiences throughout the nation alongside her adoptive mother. Ms. Ereka Howard has been recognized as an authority on motivation, peak performance, and peer leadership which has made her well respected amongst her community and audience. Ms. Ereka Howard creates an authentic connection with her audience as they think, laugh, applaud and remain engaged. Due to her ability to relate to and transform people's lives, she is a highly regarded nationally sought-after speaker. Ms. Ereka Howard displays knowledge, wisdom, and engaging speaking styles riddled with humor and captivating stories which have made her an asset to partnerships and audiences. After overcoming many hurdles throughout her life, Ms. Ereka Howard now shares her life experiences and teaches the community how to be successful throughout life. Ms. Ereka Howard has dedicated her life to the empowerment of everyone. She is a fresh voice for a new generation. Ms. Ereka Howard has a Bachelor of Science in Exercise and Sports Science and a Master in Clinical Mental Health Counseling. Ereka is currently working on a Doctorate in Counseling Education and Supervision.

Email:
mserekahoward@gmail.com
Facebook Page:
https://www.facebook.com/erekahowardmotivationalspeaker
Instagram:
https://www.instagram.com/msmotivational/
LinkedIn:
https://www.linkedin.com/in/mserekahoward/